PARKLAND

ANDY GOLDSWORTHY

YORKSHIRE SCULPTURE PARK

Parkland was originally published in 1988 to document
ephemeral work made during Andy Goldsworthy's residency at
Yorkshire Sculpture Park. In the years since its publication, Goldsworthy
has worked extensively across the world, establishing
an international reputation.

In 2007 Andy Goldsworthy returns to stage the largest and most ambitious
project ever curated at Yorkshire Sculpture Park, including major permanent works
in the landscape. Parkland has been reprinted in celebration of the journey taken
by both artist and organisation.

Designed by Andy Goldsworthy and Donato Cinicolo 3

Published by Yorkshire Sculpture Park in 1988
Reprinted in 2007

Andy Goldsworthy is represented by Galerie Lelong, New York, USA;
Galerie Lelong, Paris, France; Haines Gallery, San Francisco, USA;
Michael Hue-Williams Fine Art (Albion Gallery), London, UK;
Springer & Winckler Galerie, Berlin, Germany; Galerie S65, Aalst, Belgium.

ISBN 1 871480 58 2

Yorkshire Sculpture Park receives funding from Arts Council England,
Wakefield Metropolitan District Council, and West Yorkshire Grants (a joint committee
of Bradford, Calderdale, Kirklees, Leeds and Wakefield Councils).

A VISIT IN EACH SEASON
THREE MONTHS' WORK
YORKSHIRE SCULPTURE PARK
1987

WINTER

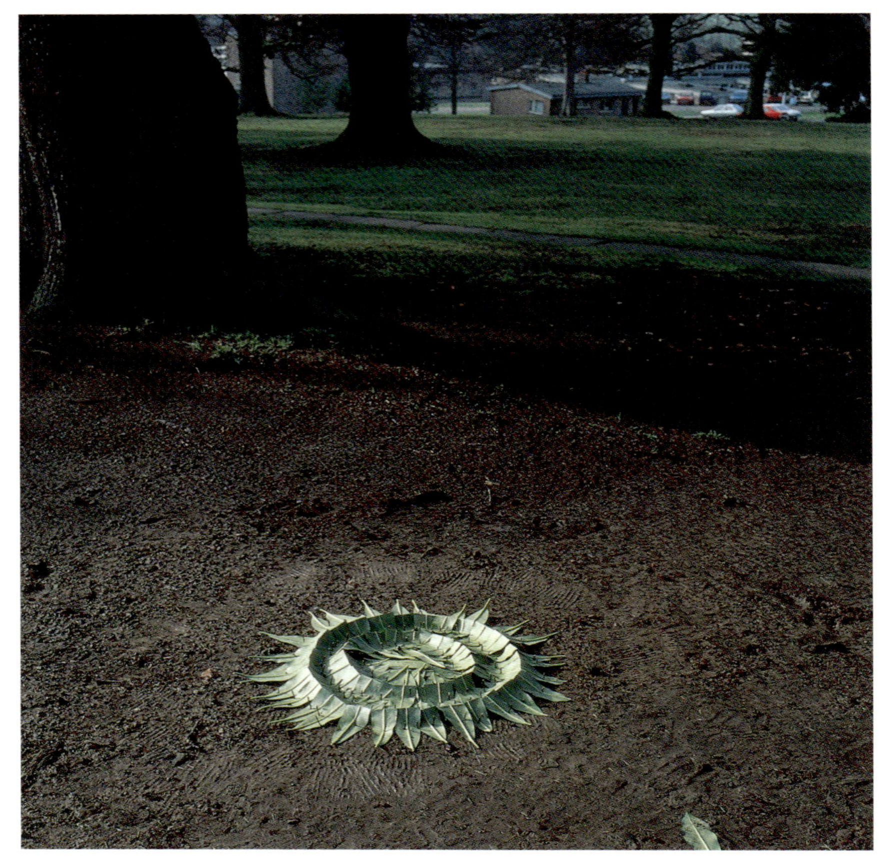

Rhododendron leaves
creased to catch the hazy to bright light
held to the ground with thorns

11 FEBRUARY 1987

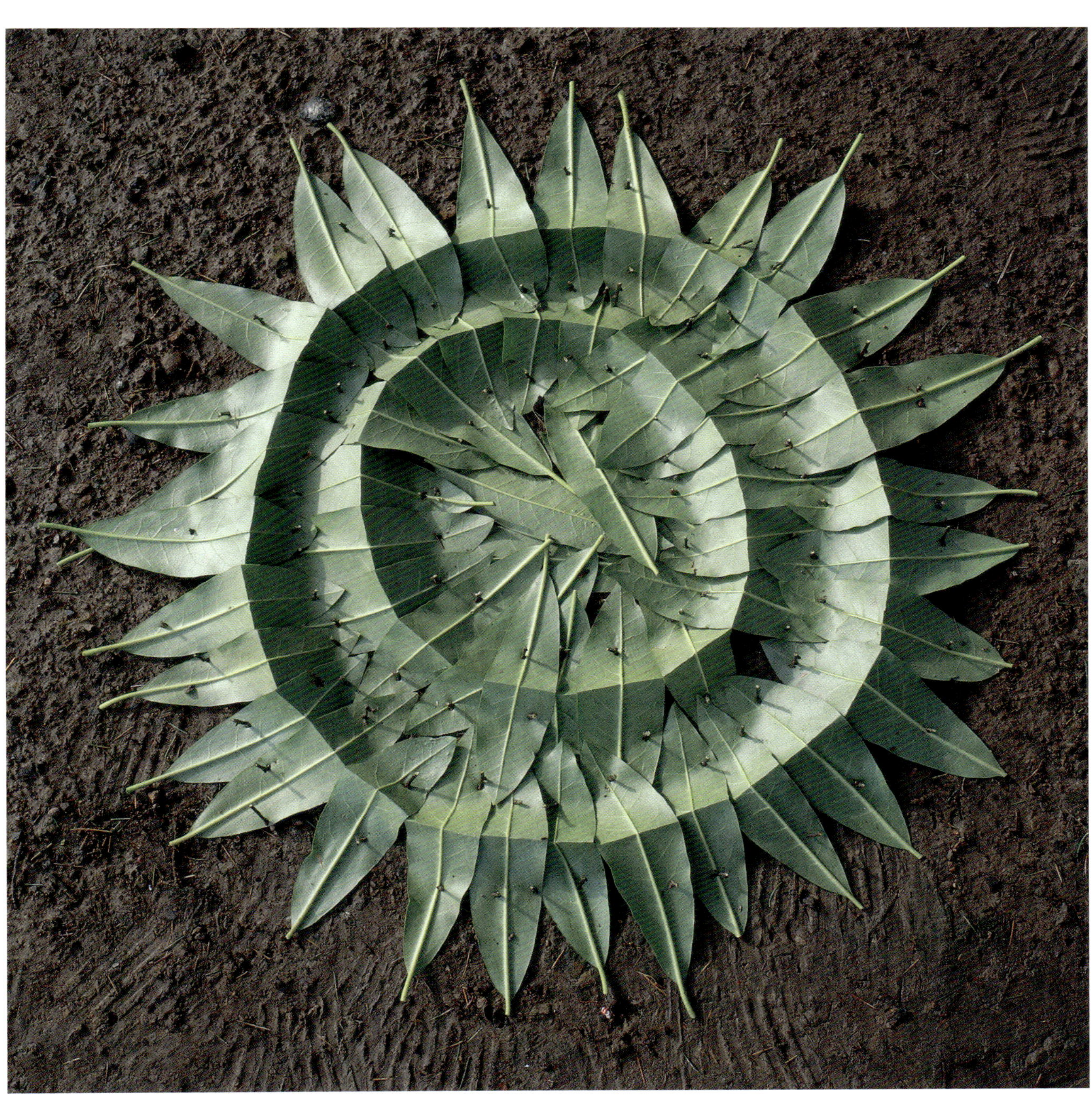

Broken ice
remains of several failed works
laid in sun and shadows
quickly melting

15 FEBRUARY 1987

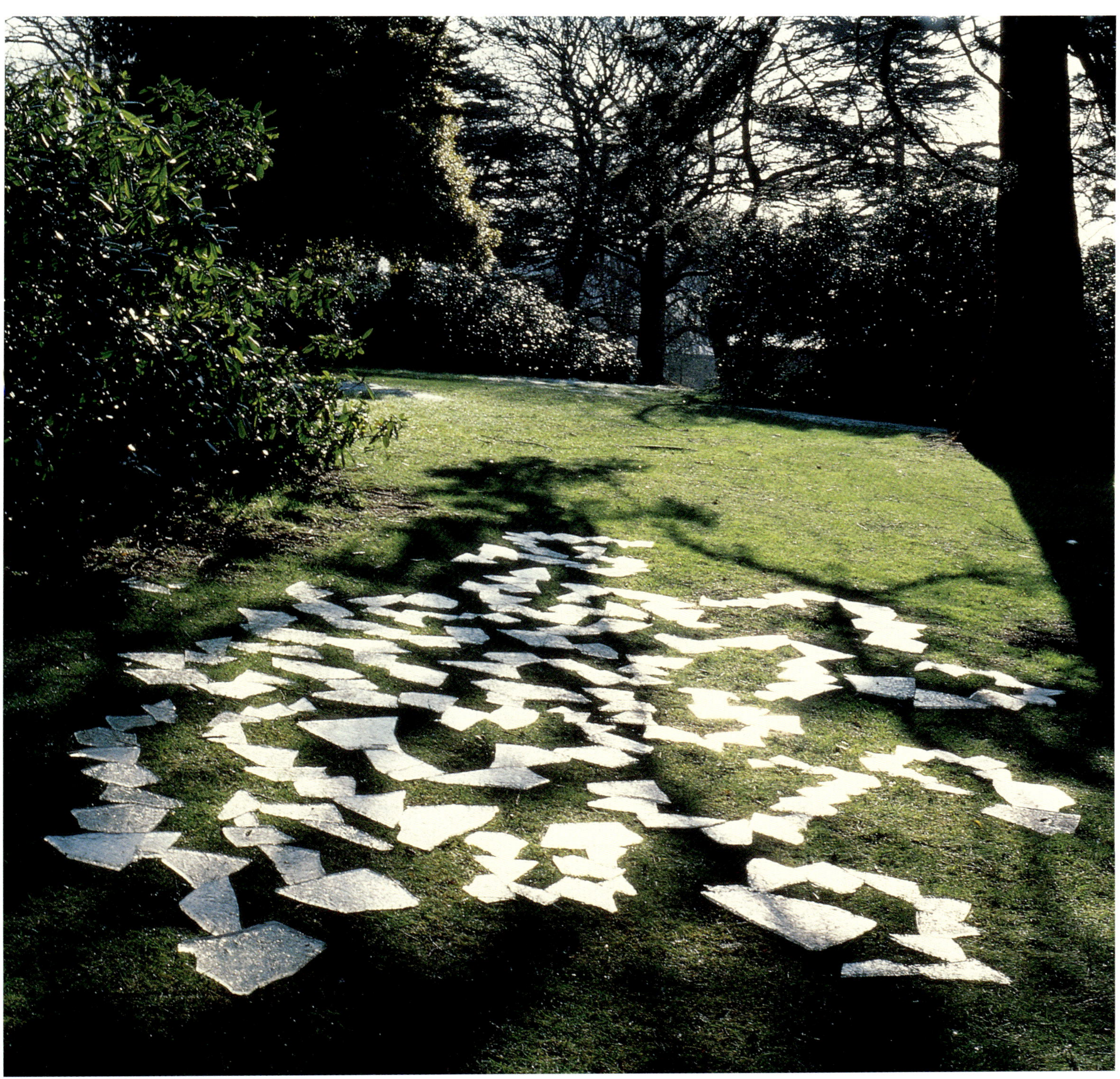

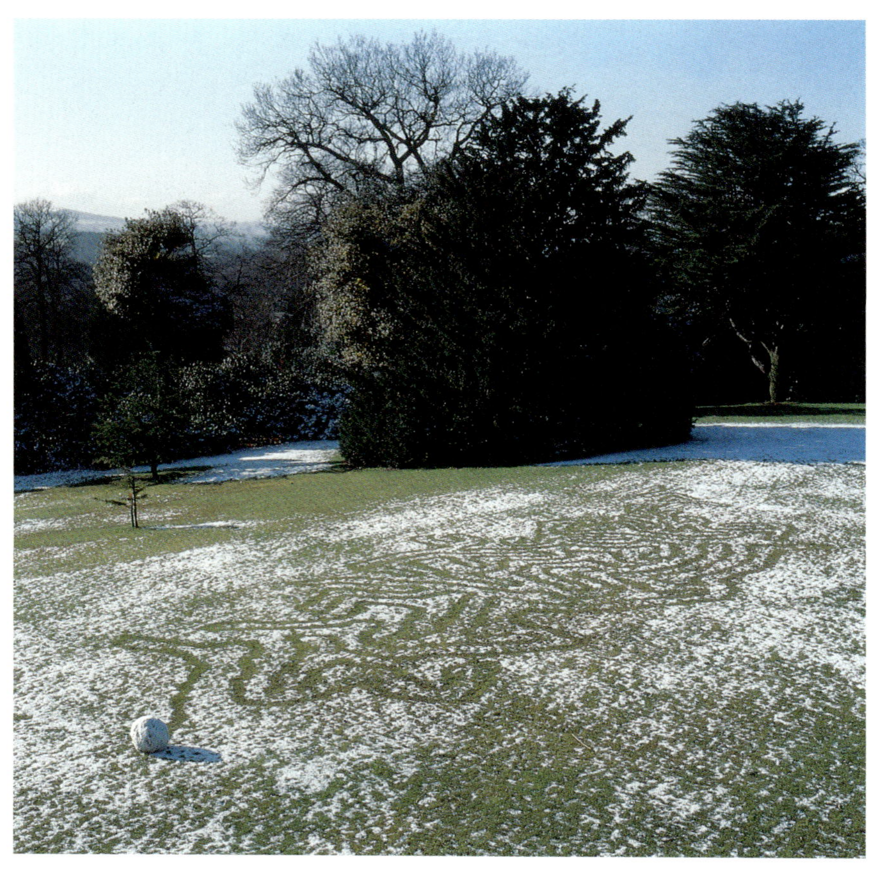

Thin covering of snow
melting
rolled a snowball
quickly

15 FEBRUARY 1987

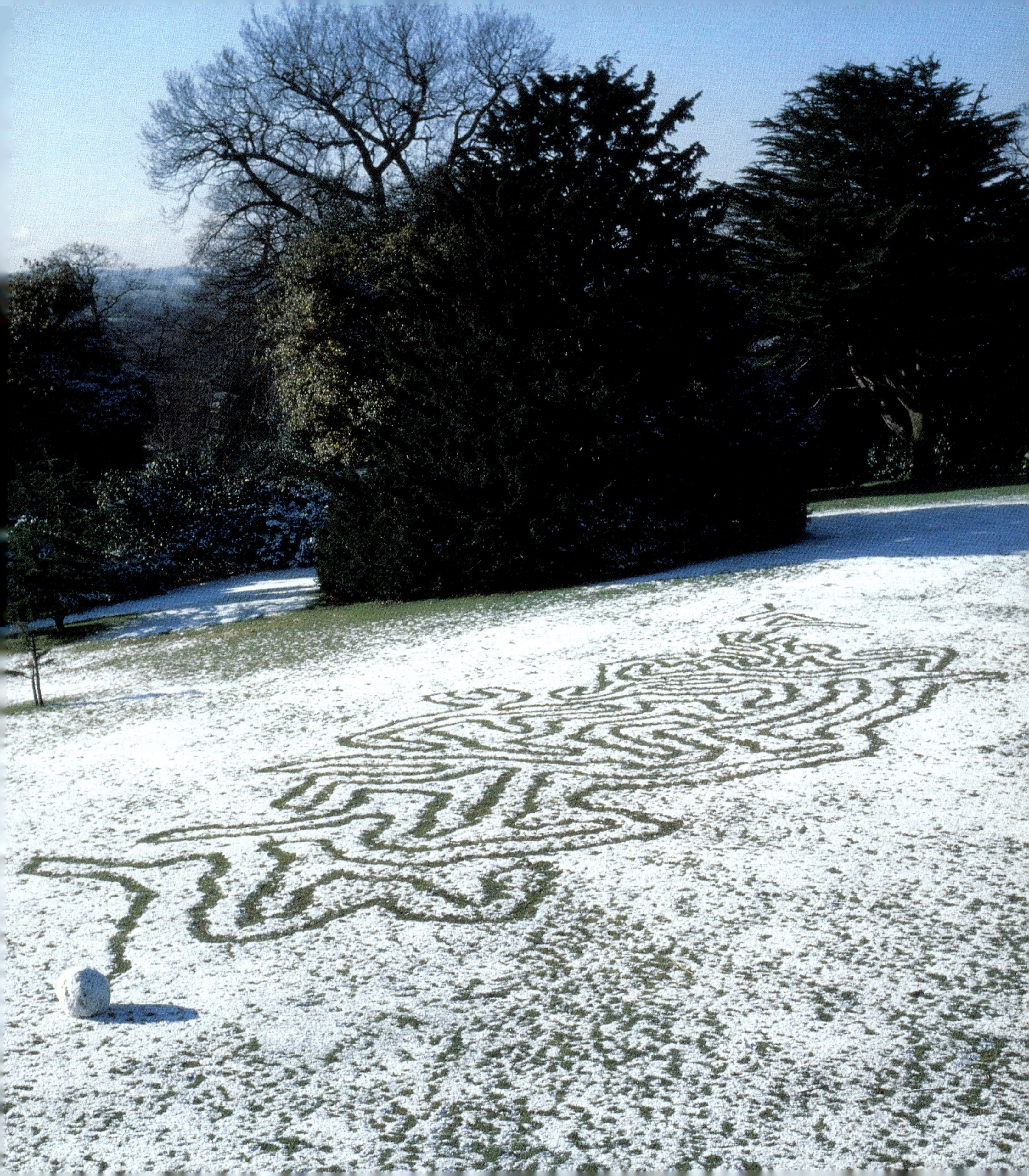

Worked through the night
working the cold
only just below freezing
difficult to make ice stick
held each piece until frozen
pouring water over to make it more solid
occasionally letting go too soon
often causing several pieces to fall
work finished as dawn broke
no longer cold enough

17 FEBRUARY 1987

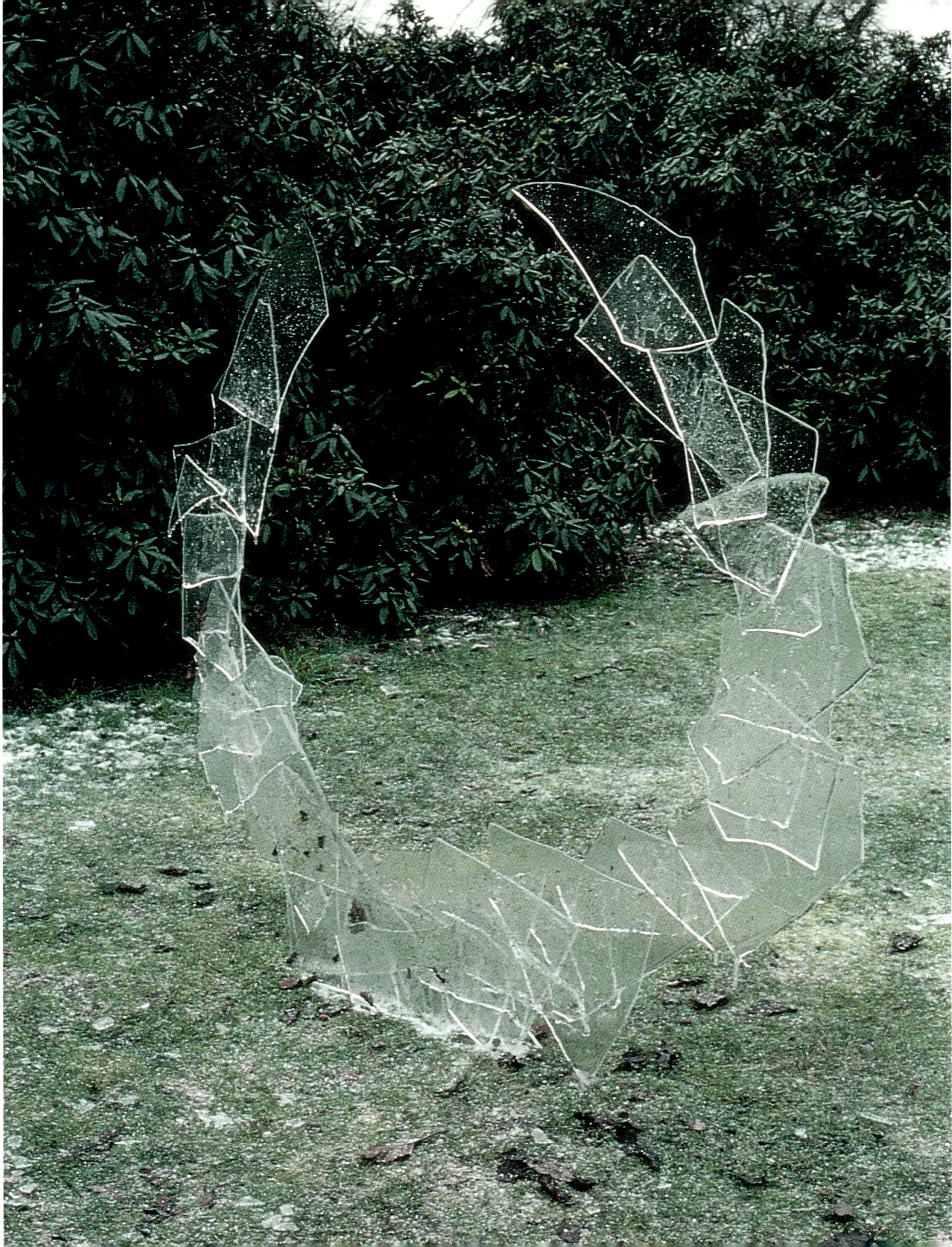

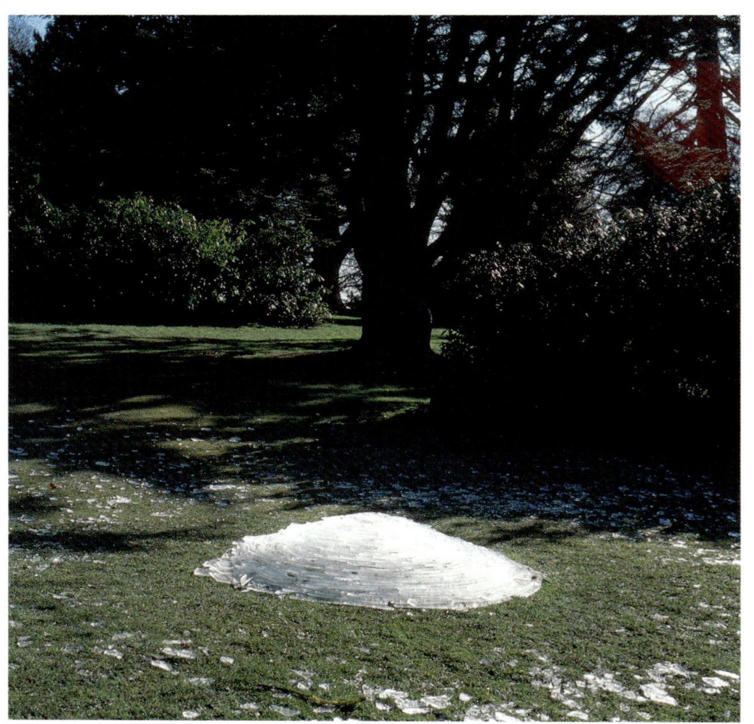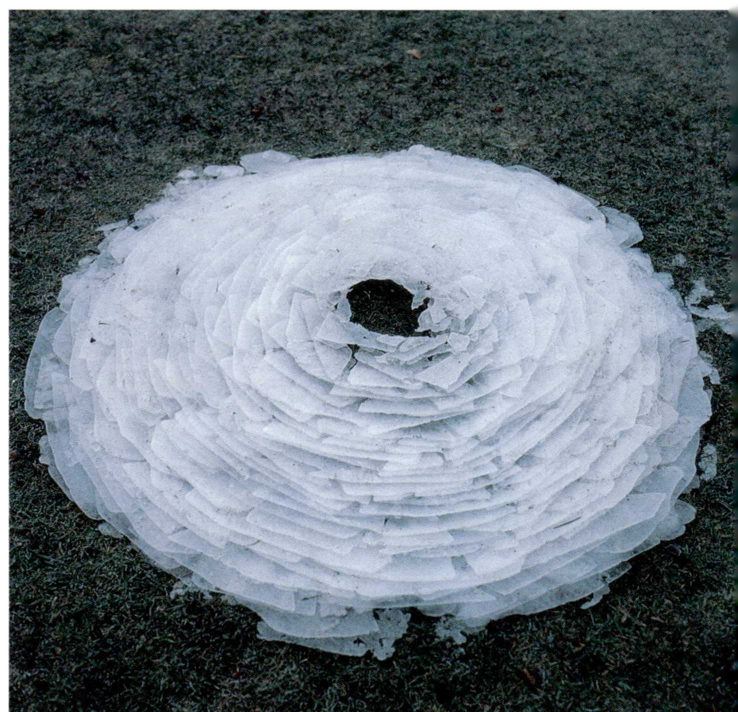

Worked through the night
clear and freezing to begin with
banks of clouds drifting over
became warmer, difficult to work
several things collapsed
struggling
began to make ice/mound/hole
finished before the sun came up
lasted several days
freezing at night, thawing during the day
growing smaller

20 FEBRUARY 1987

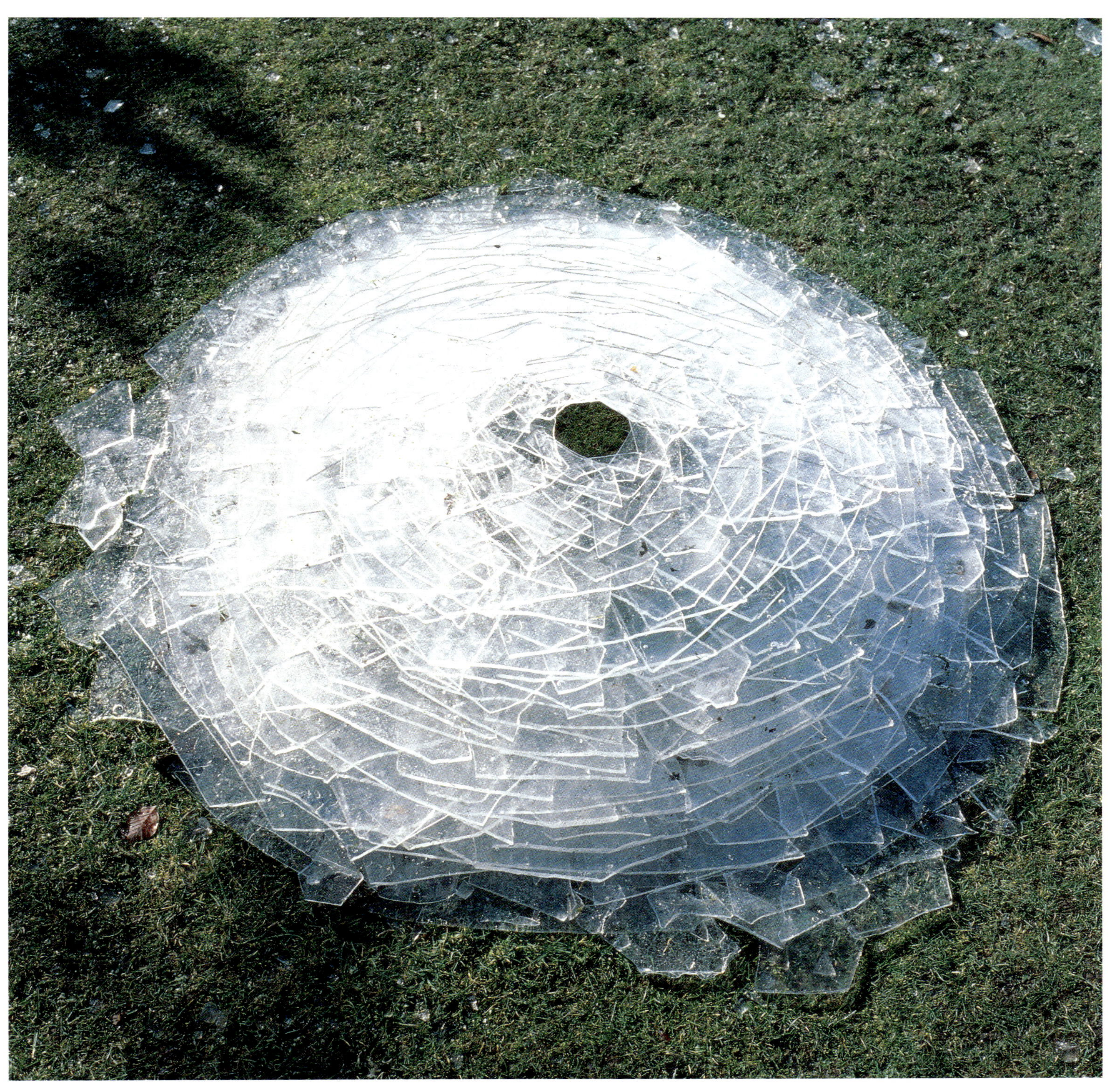

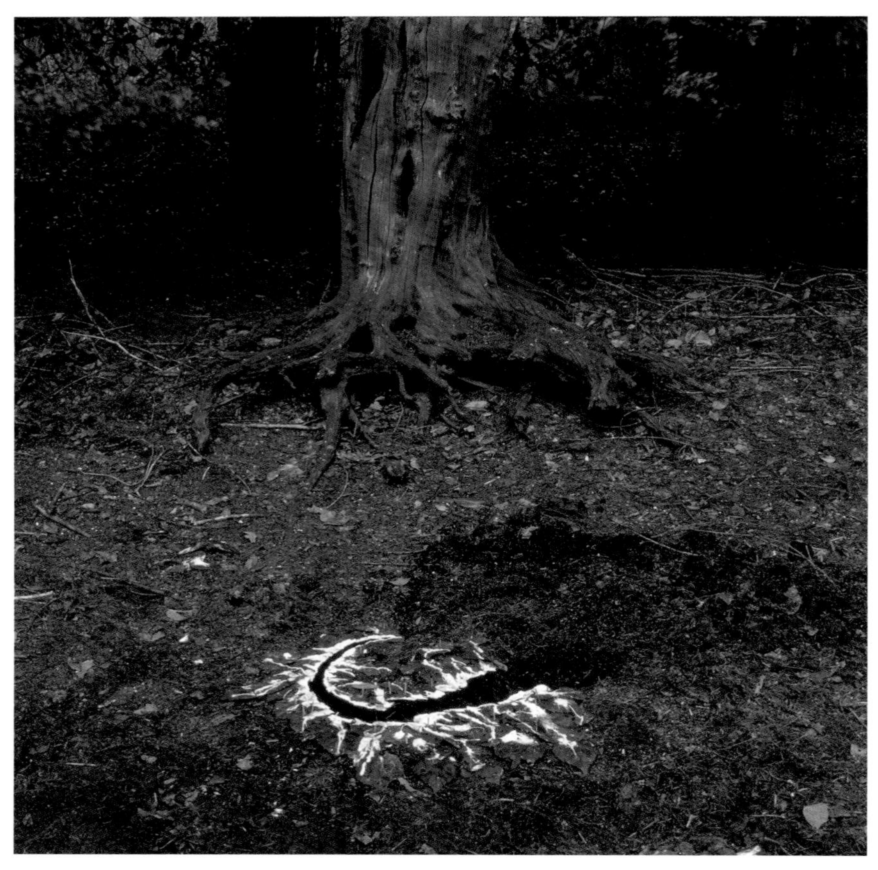

Blackberry leaves
splattered white with bird droppings after a few days of little rain
collected splashes
laid alongside a scraping
occasional dangerous showers of rain

23 FEBRUARY 1987

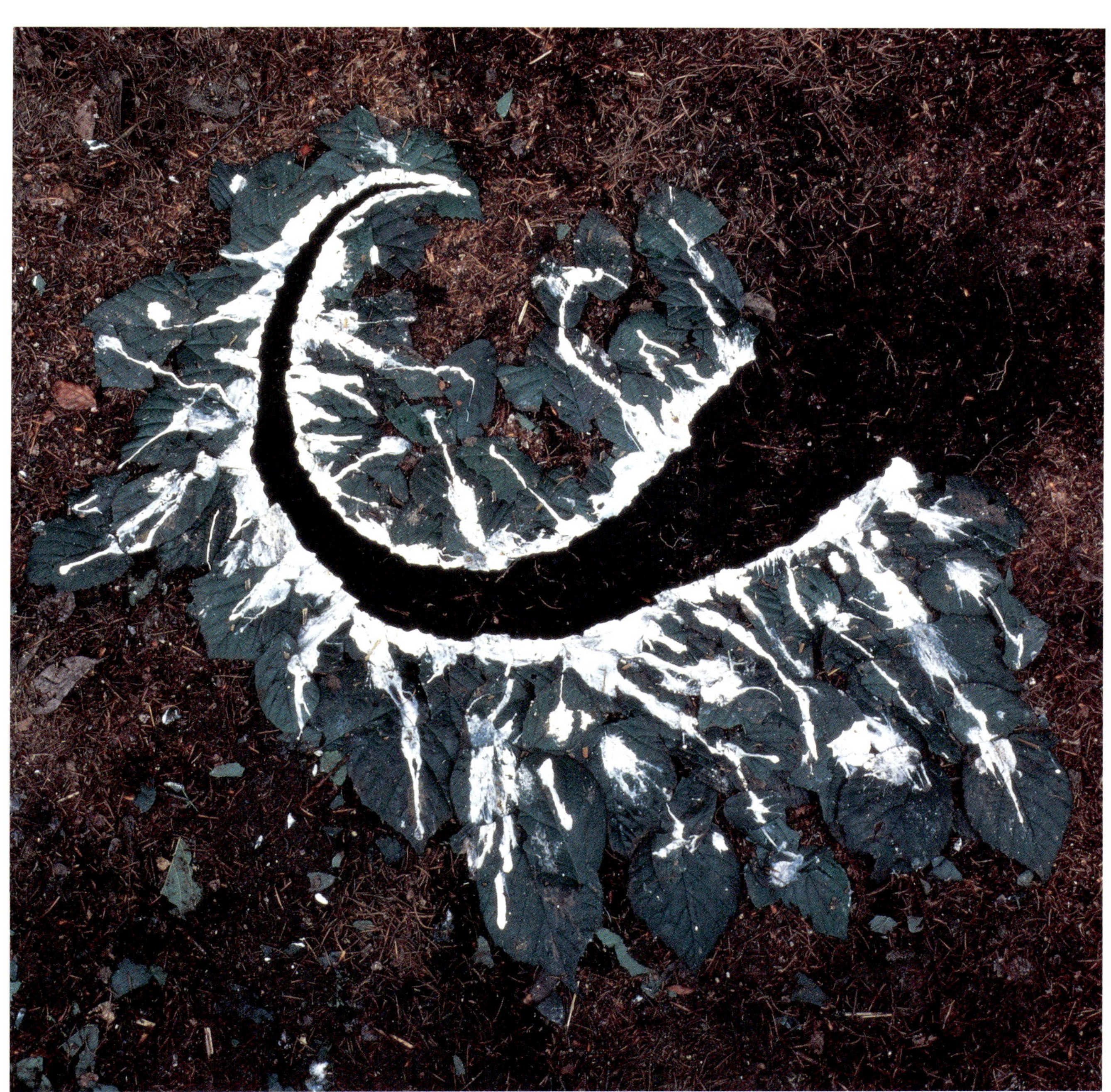

SPRING

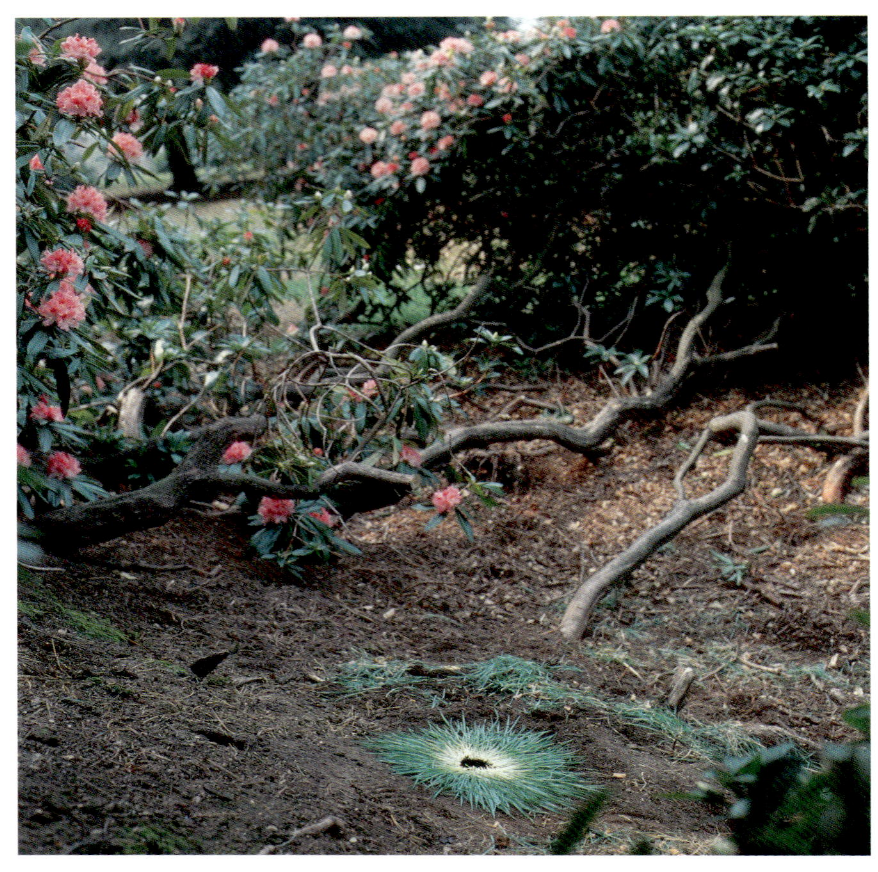

Spring grass
fresh green blades
white stems
laid around a hole

25 APRIL 1987

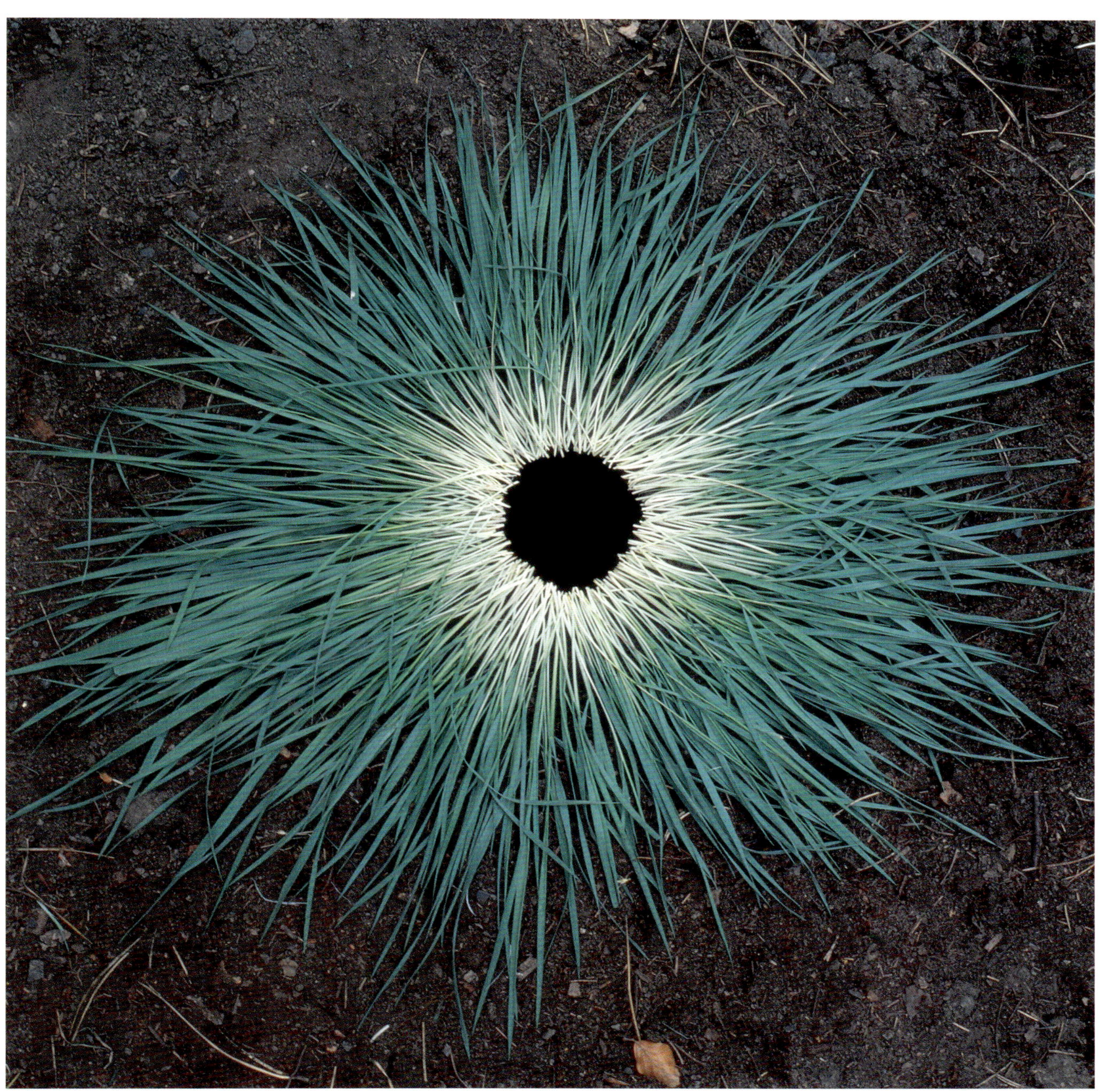

Dandelions
newly flowered
none as yet turned to seed
undamaged by wind or rain
a grass verge between dual carriageways
on the way to Bretton

28 APRIL 1987

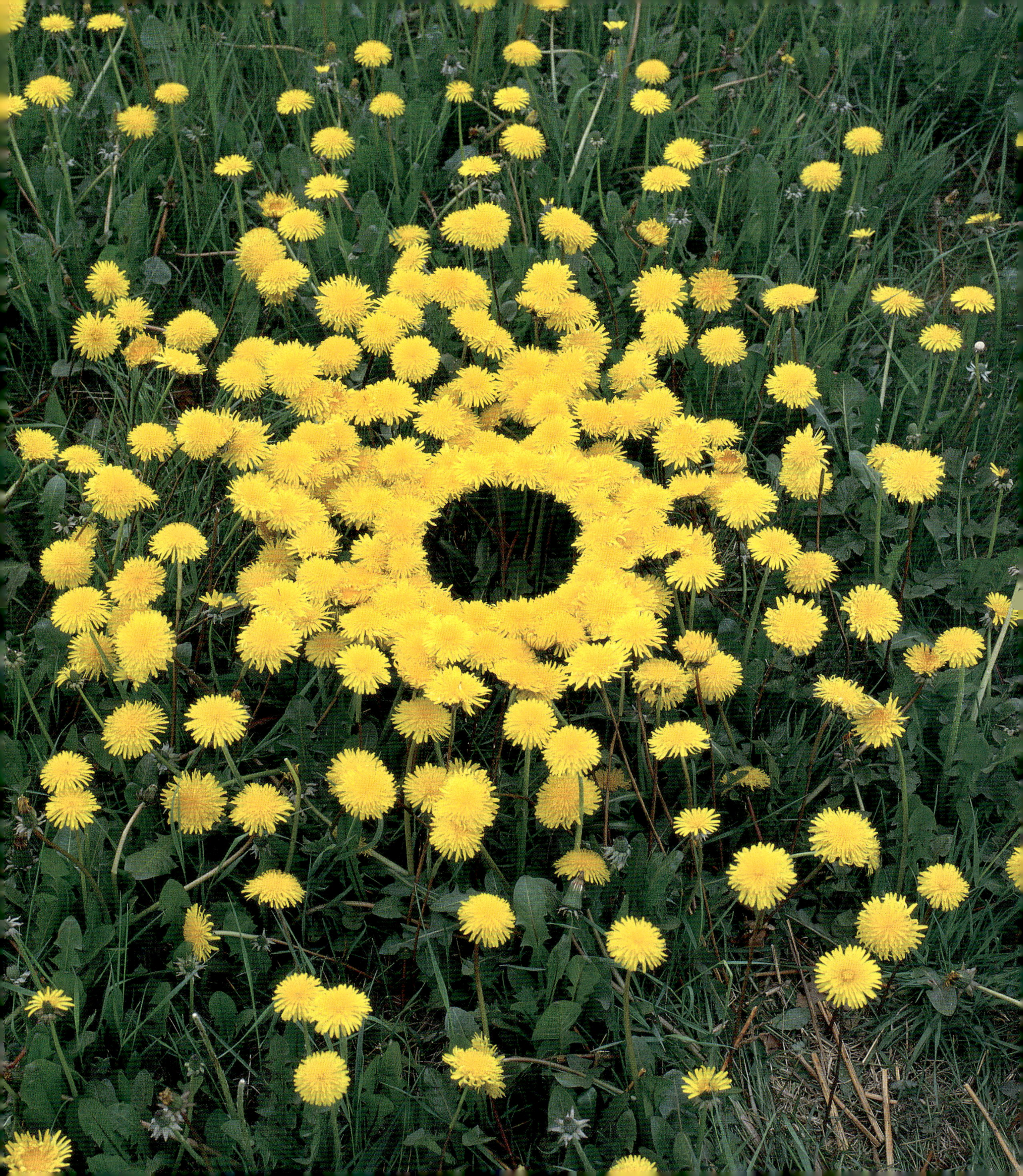

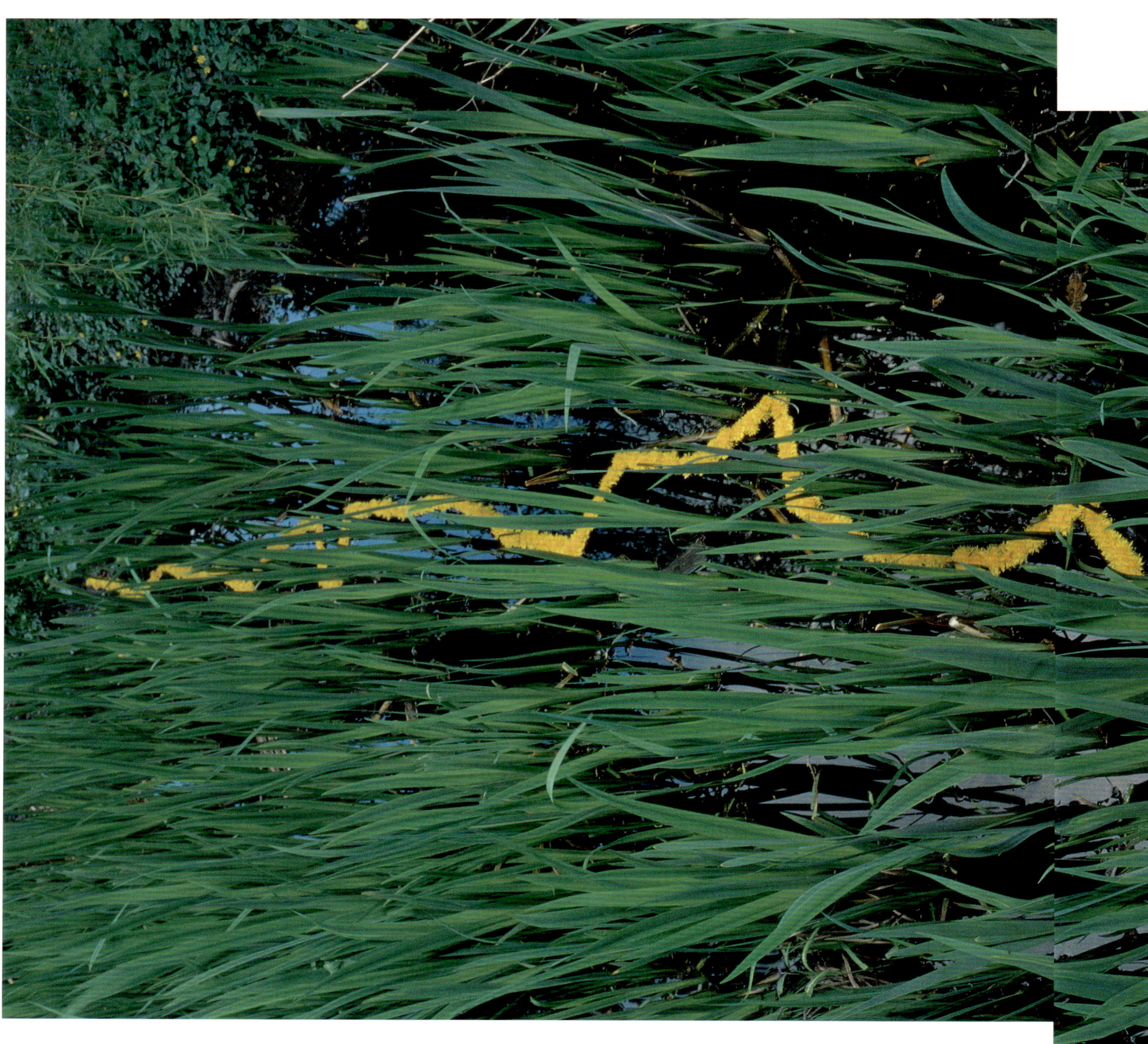

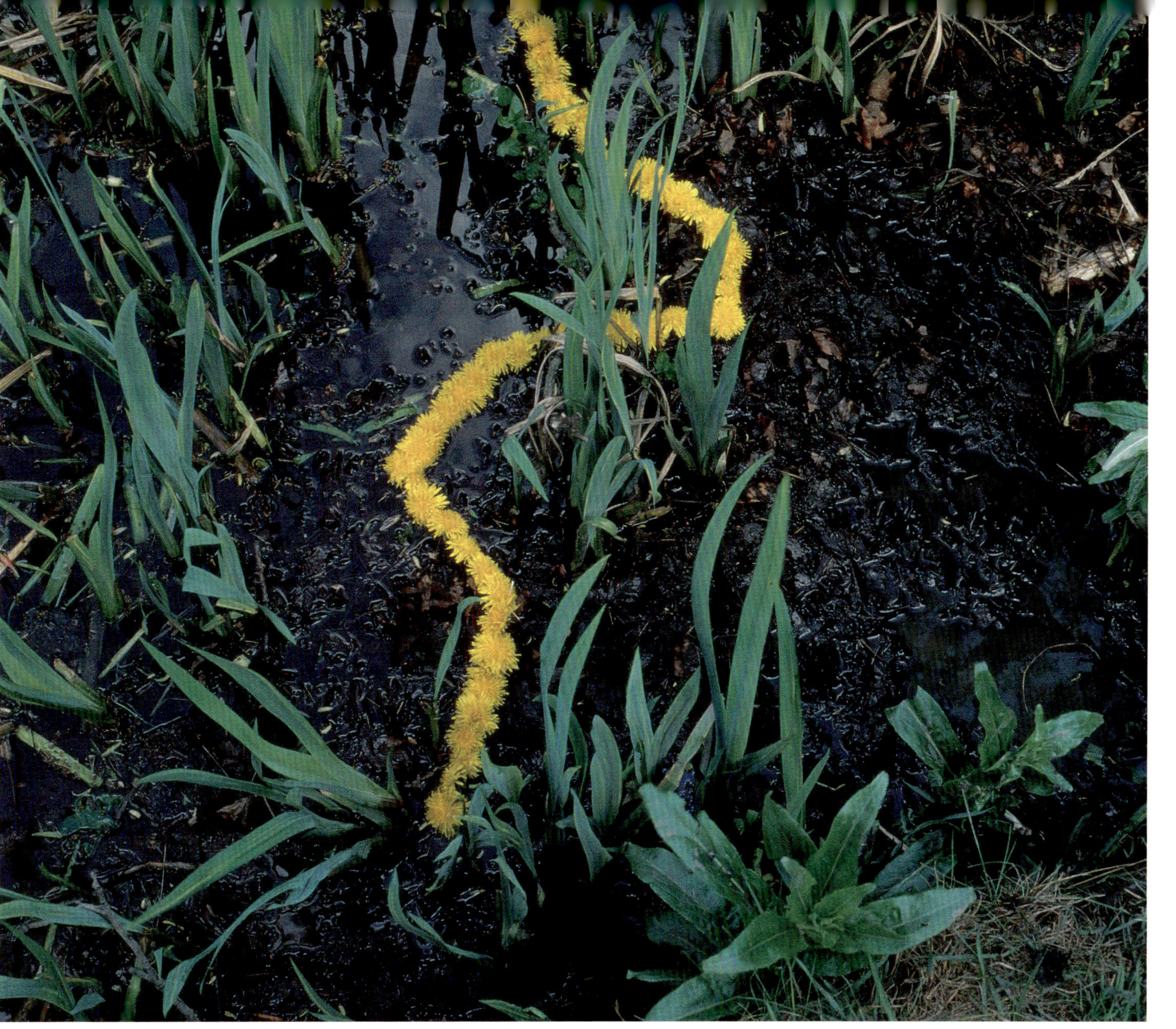

Dandelions
collected along the way to Bretton
threaded on to grass stalks
laid on the water
end to end
bright, sunny

4 MAY 1987

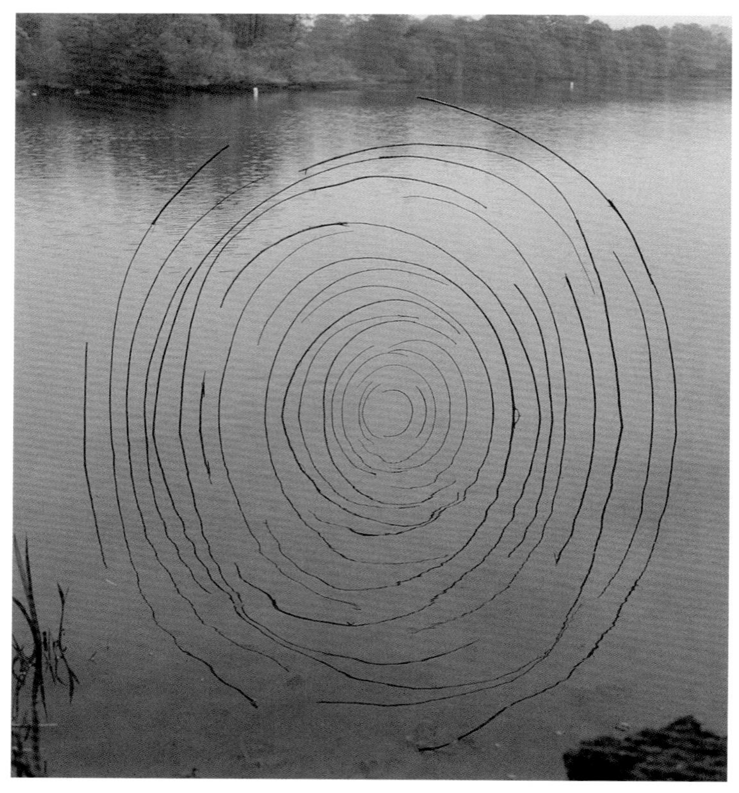

Two works made in the same place
sticks and willow herb stalks
pushed into lake bottom
shallow around the edge
both days sunny and calm to begin with
as I finished the sky darkened
breeze
ripples

29 APRIL, 3 MAY 1987

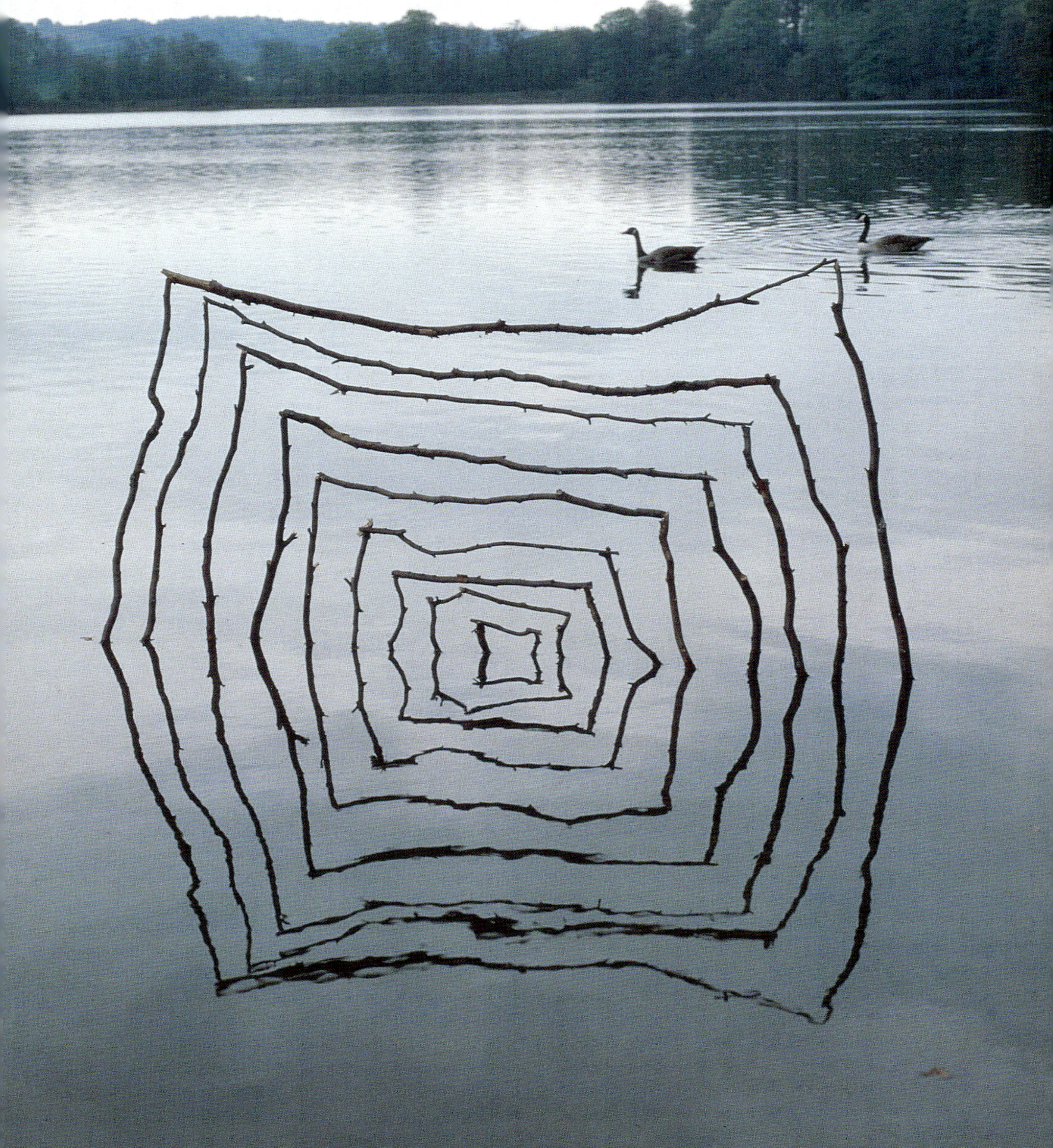

Scrapings
edged with mud
plucked dandelion petals laid along the edges
cloudy
occasional sun causing petals to shrivel

7 MAY 1987

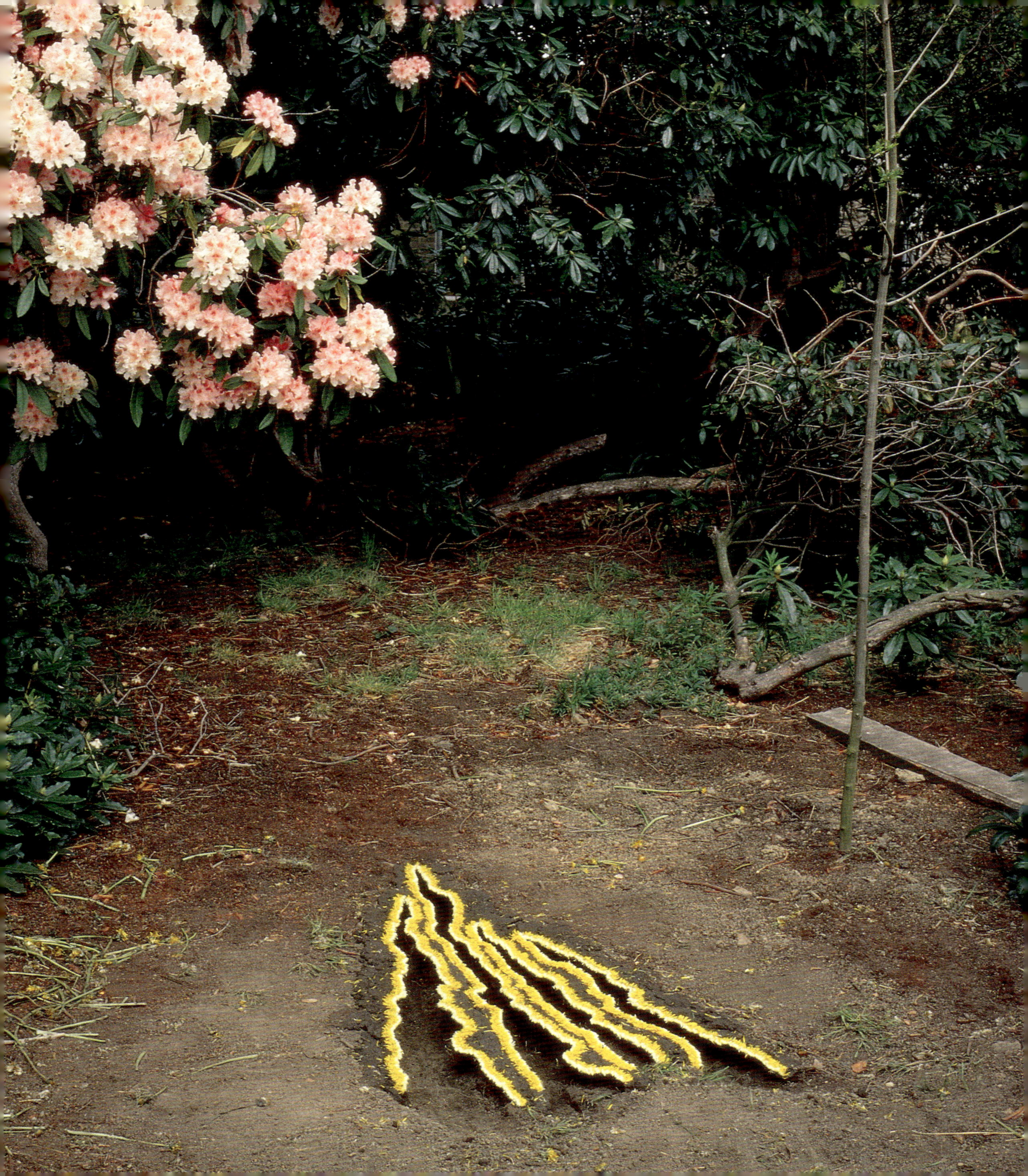

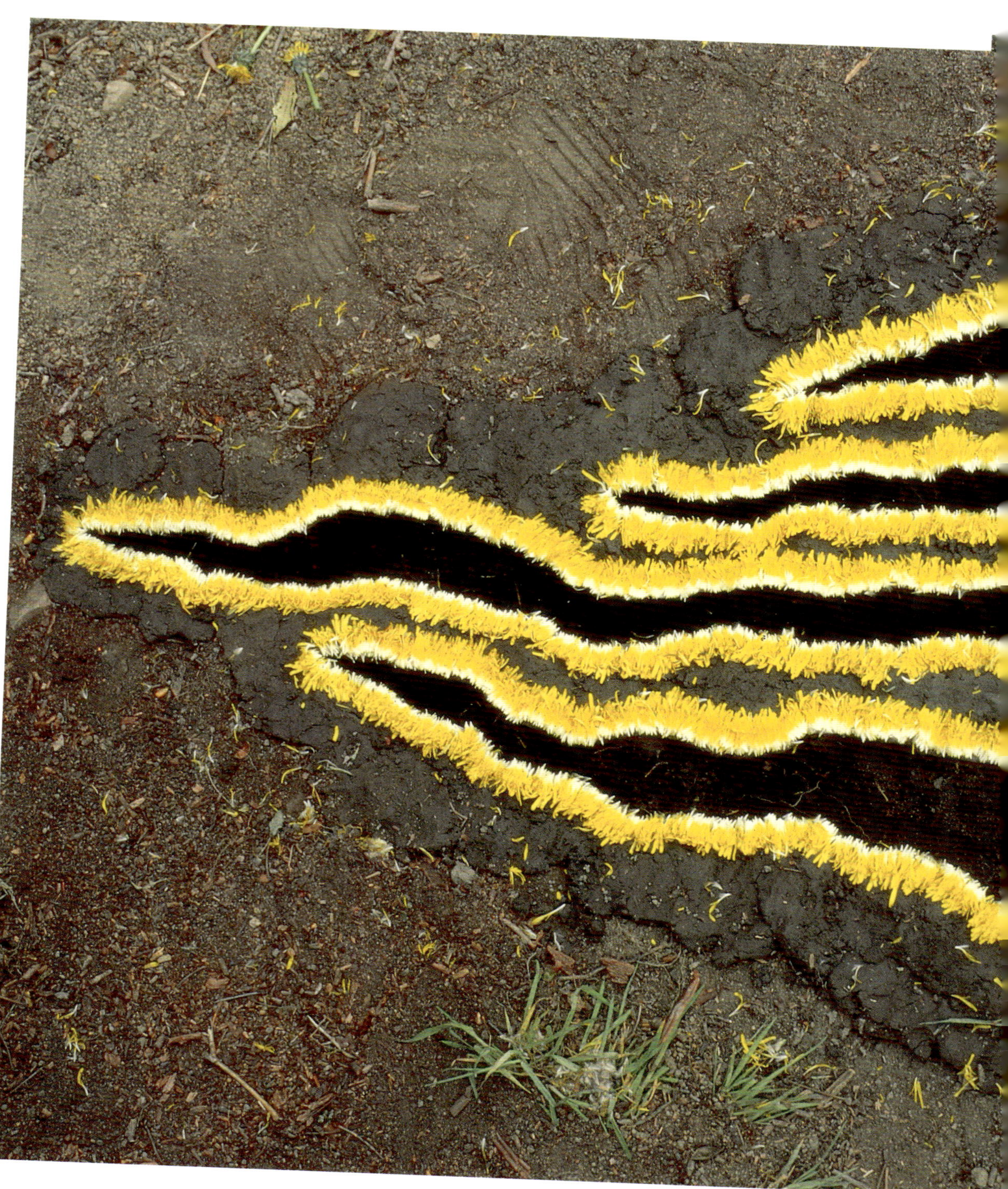

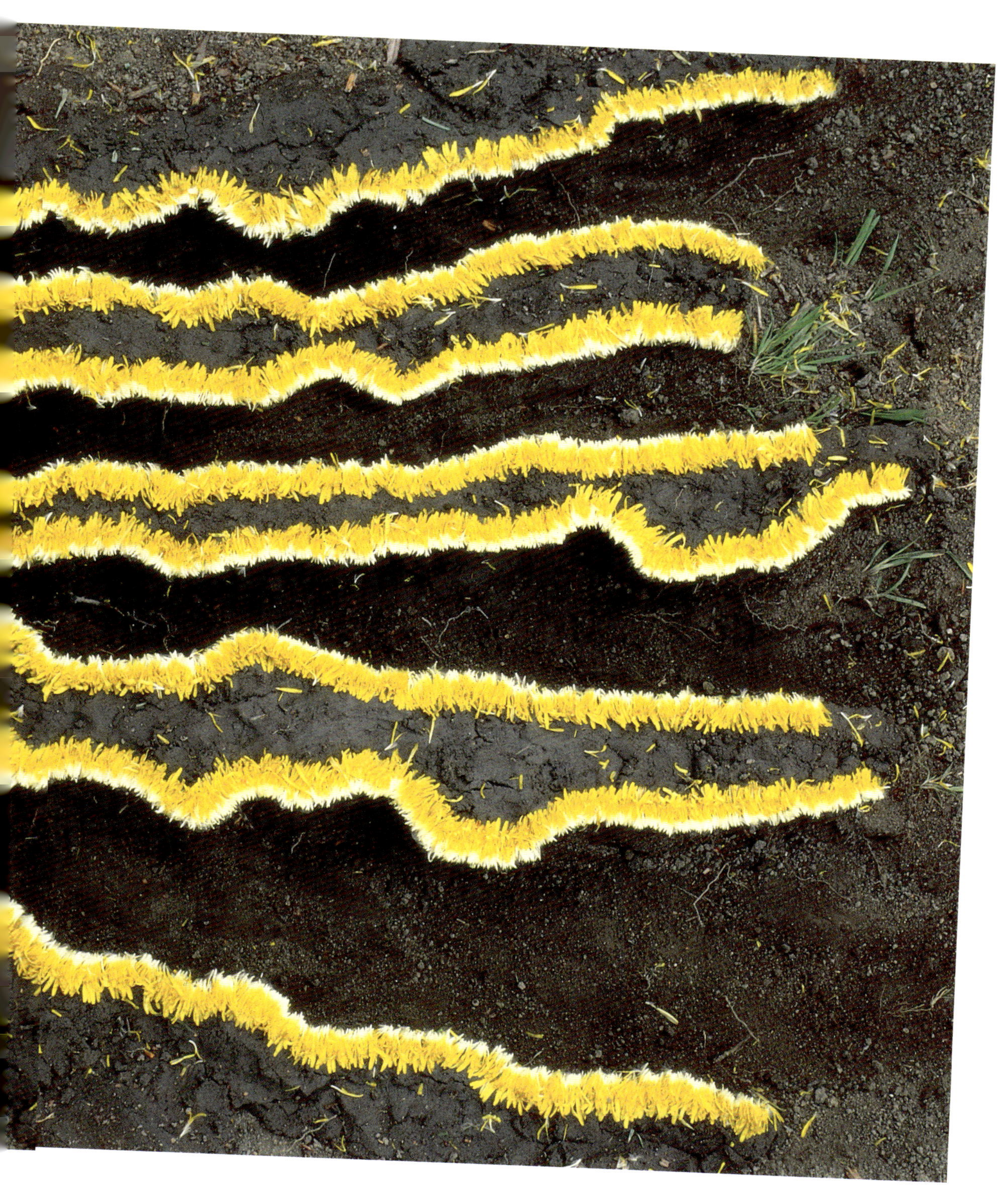

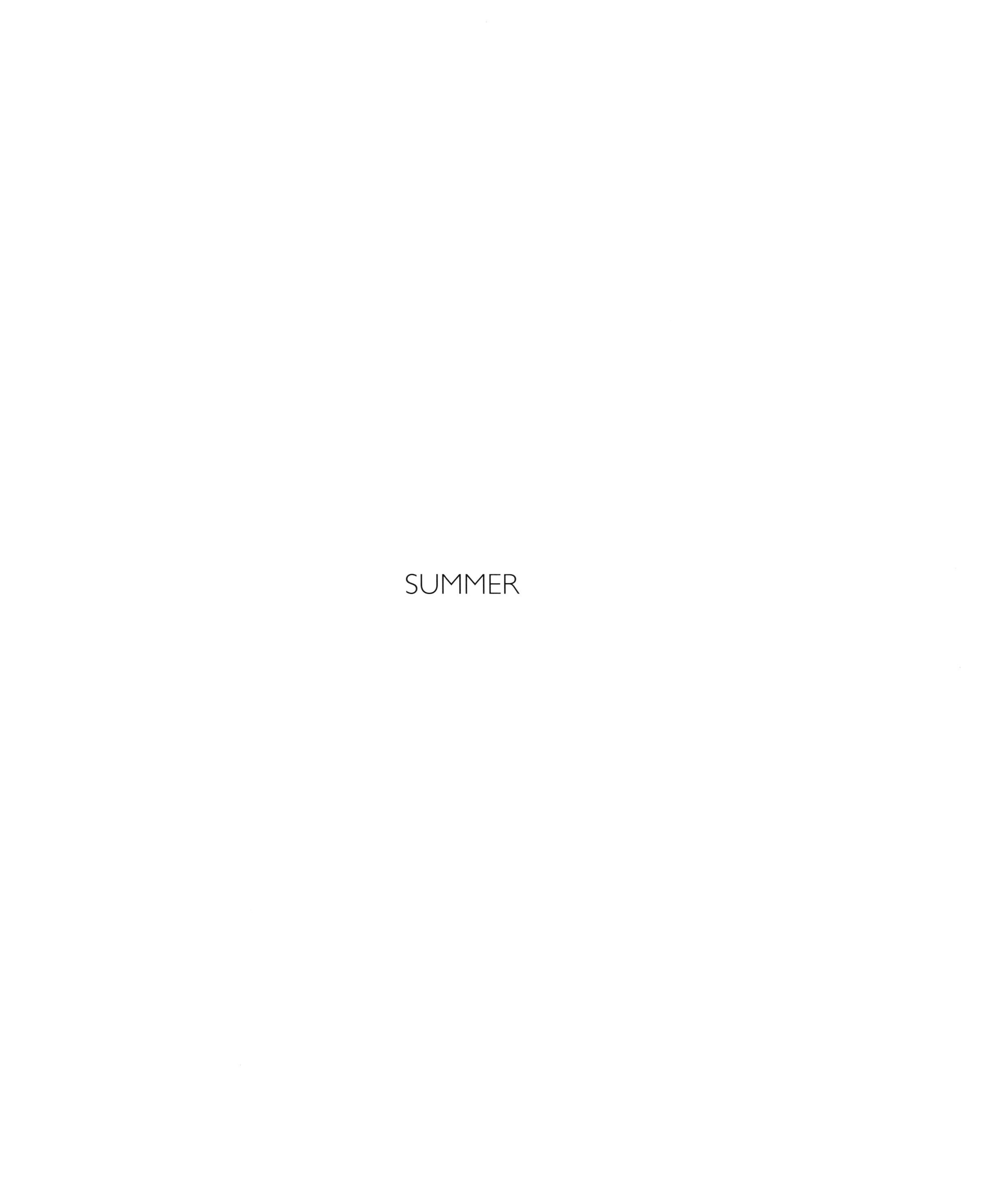

SUMMER

Sycamore leaf sections
torn out
smeared with mud
laid alongside a trench

1 AUGUST 1987

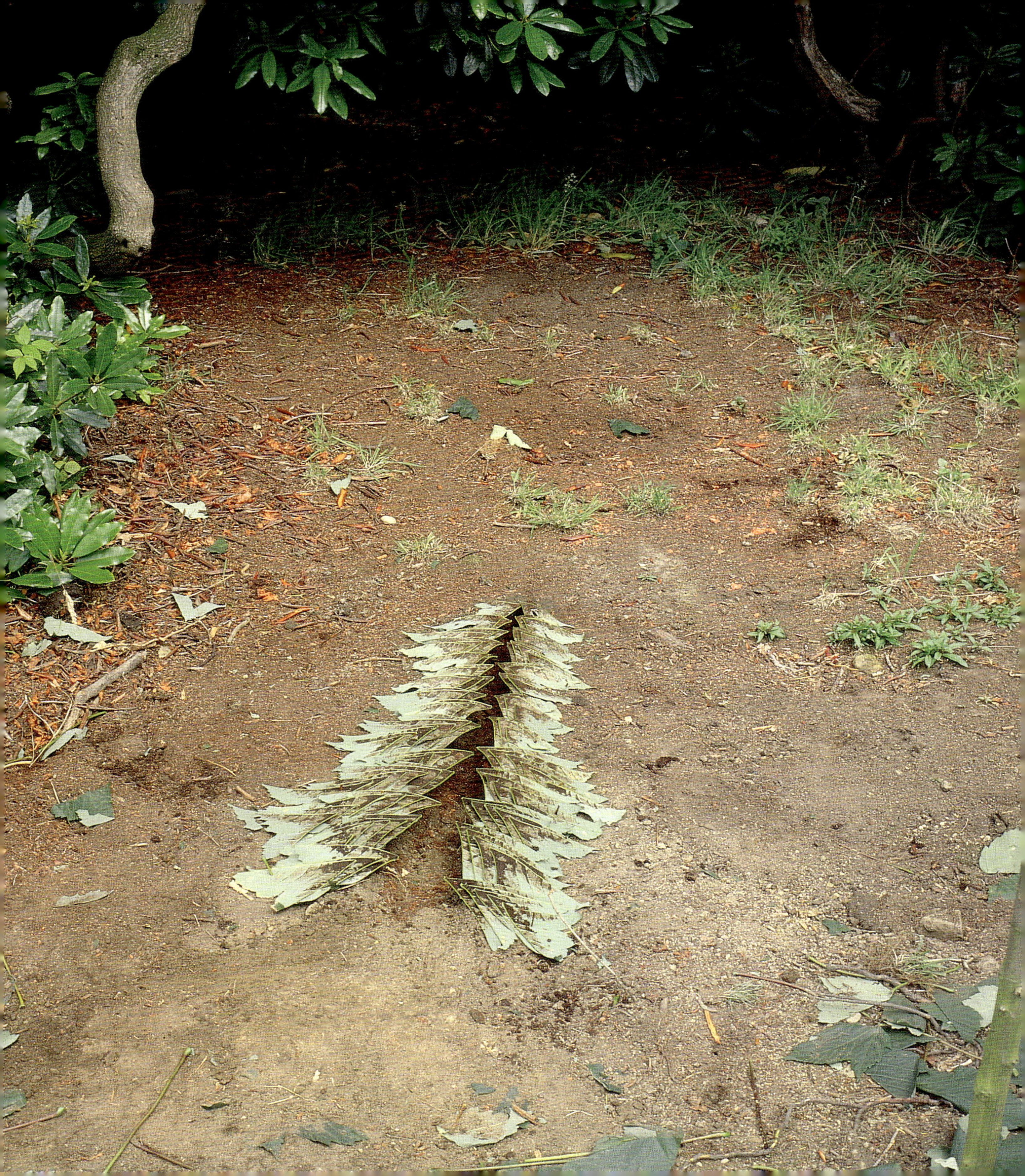

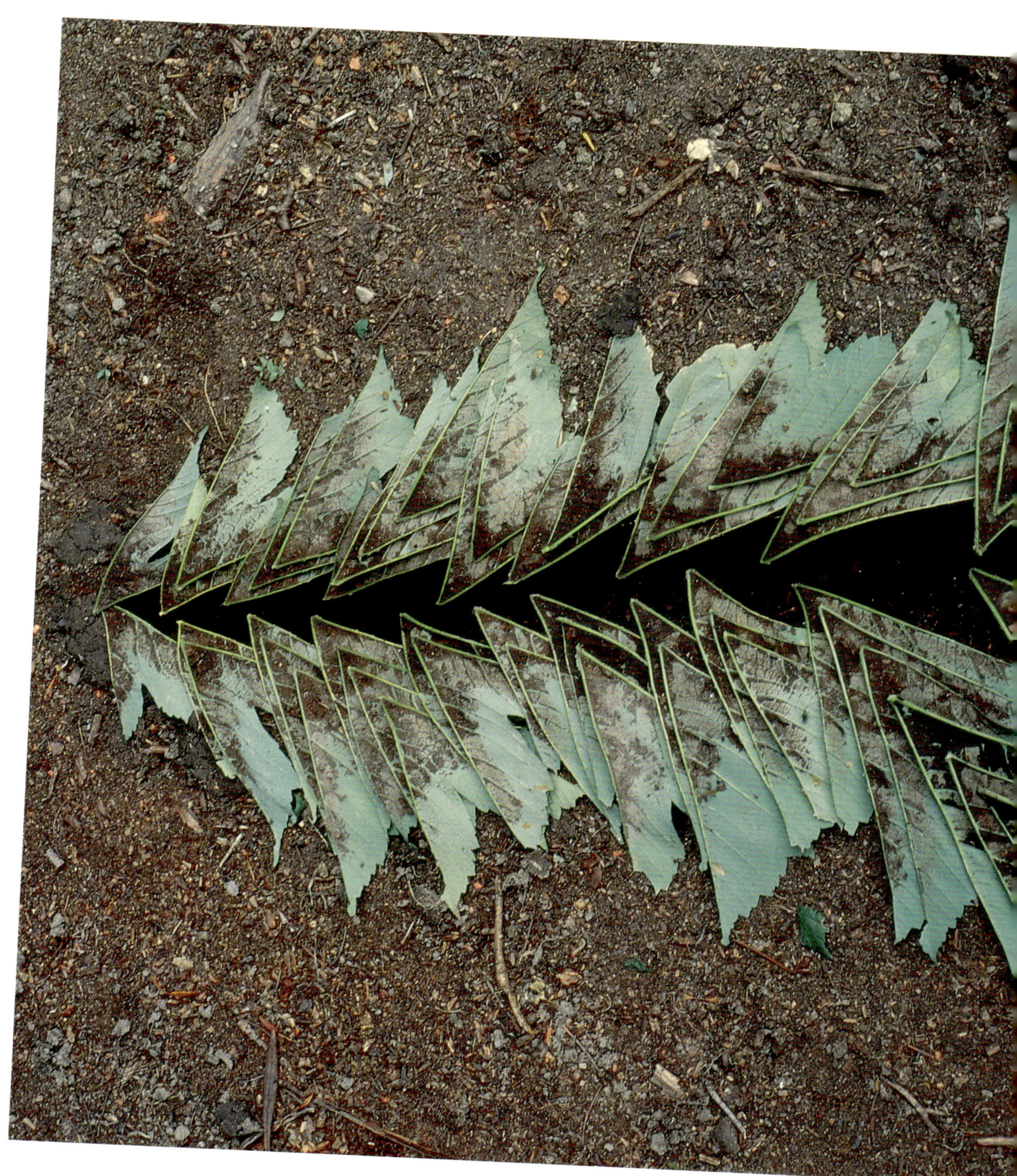

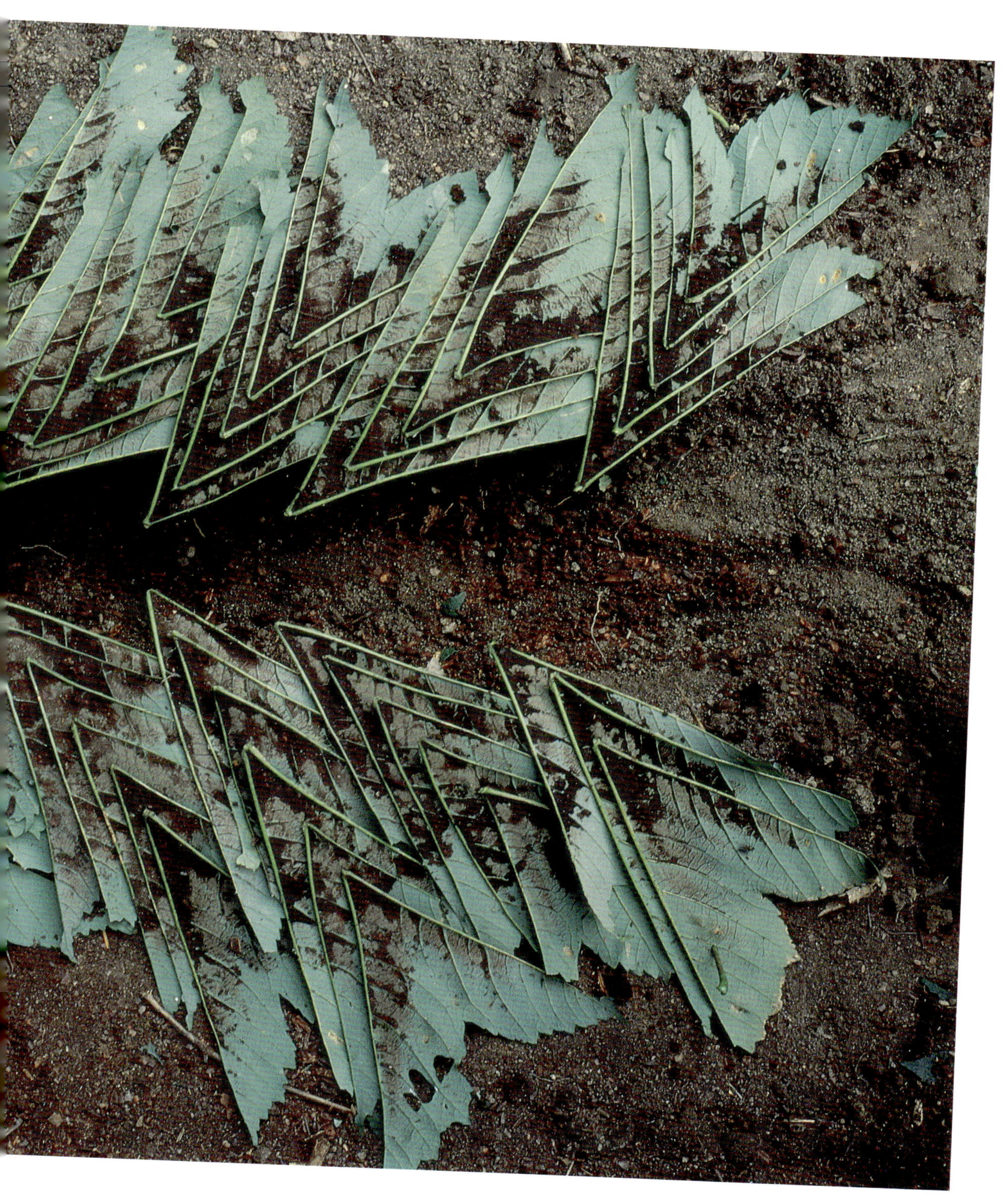

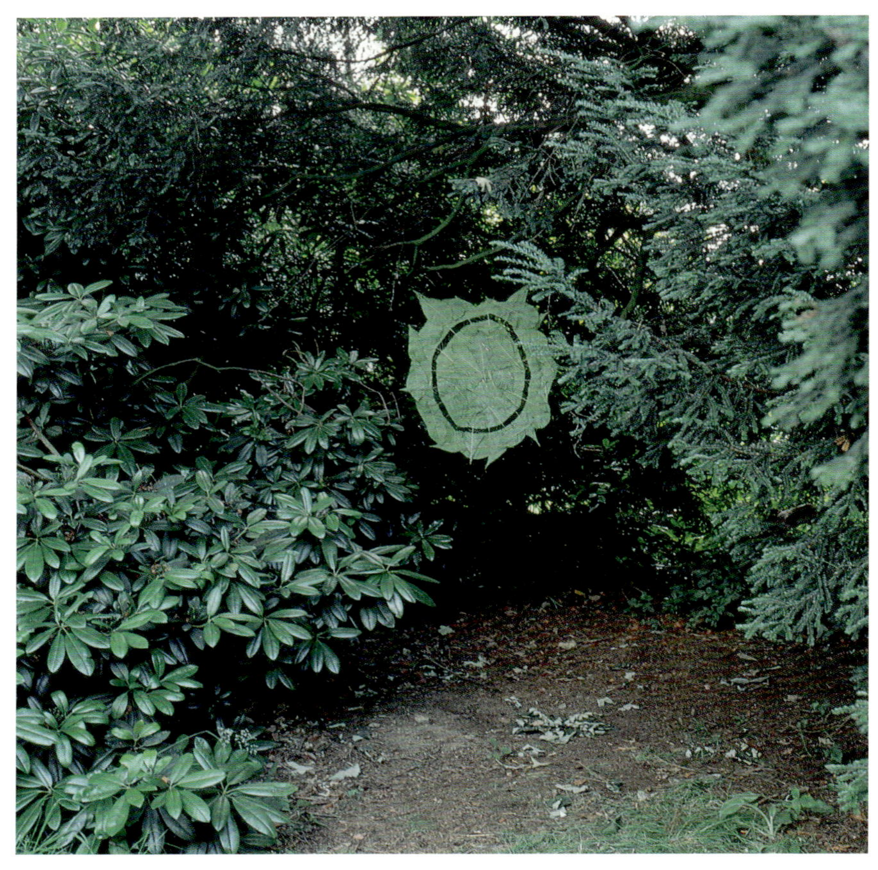

Horse chestnut leaves
sections torn out leaving the veins
stitched together with grass stalks
hung in the darkness of rhododendron and yew

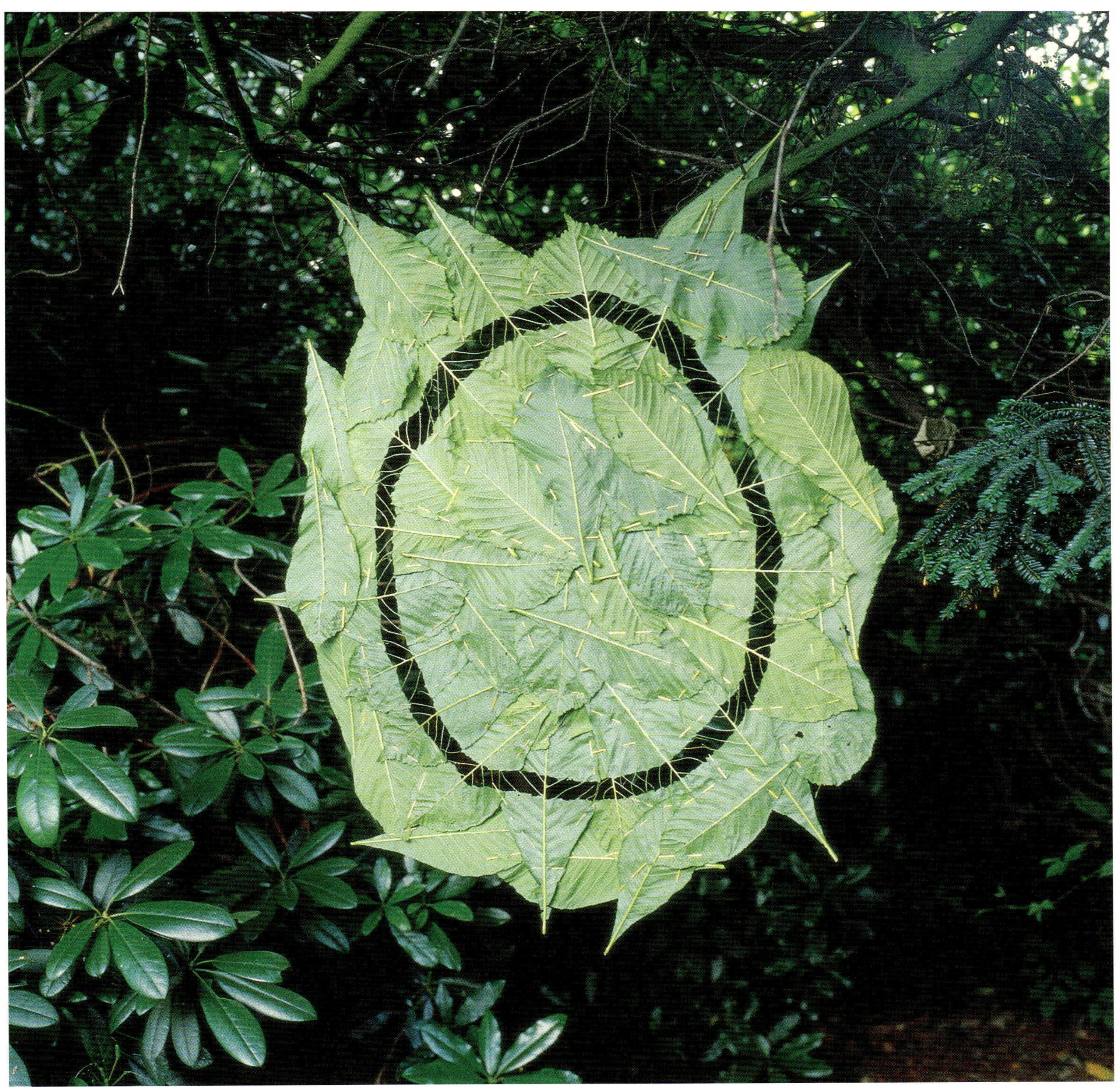

Sweet chestnut green horn
continuous spiral
each leaf laid in the fold of another
stitched with thorns

9 AUGUST 1987

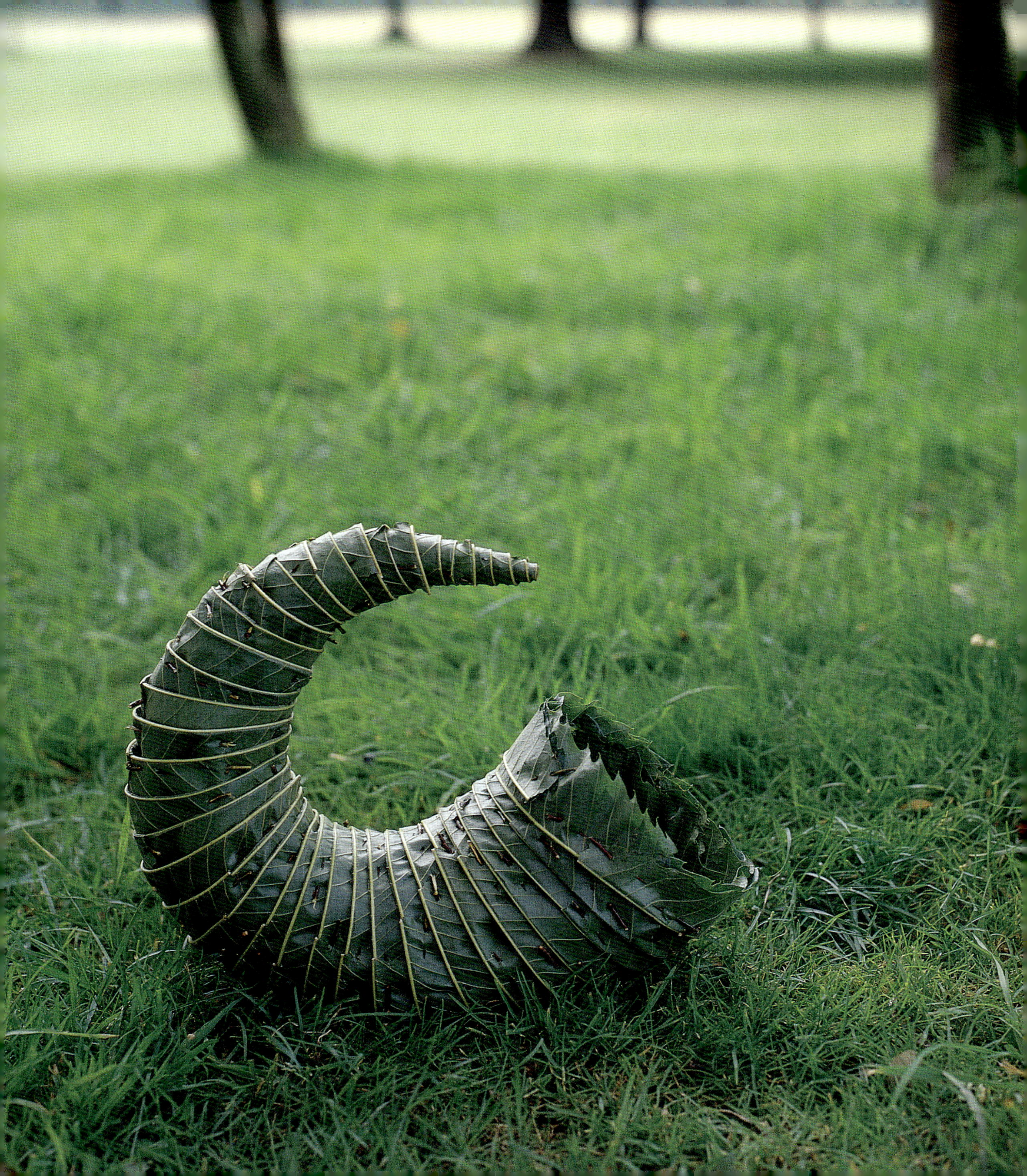

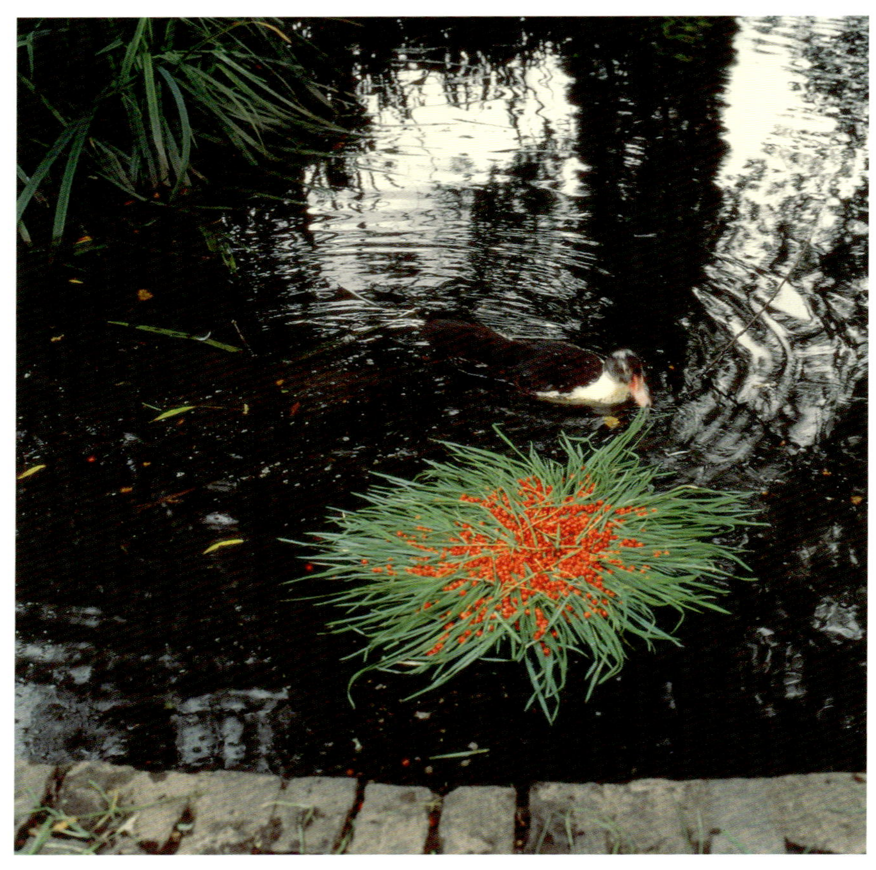

Calm overcast
laid iris blades on pond
pinned together with thorns
filled in five sections with rowan berries
fish attacking from below
difficult to keep all the berries in
nibbled at by ducks

29 AUGUST 1987

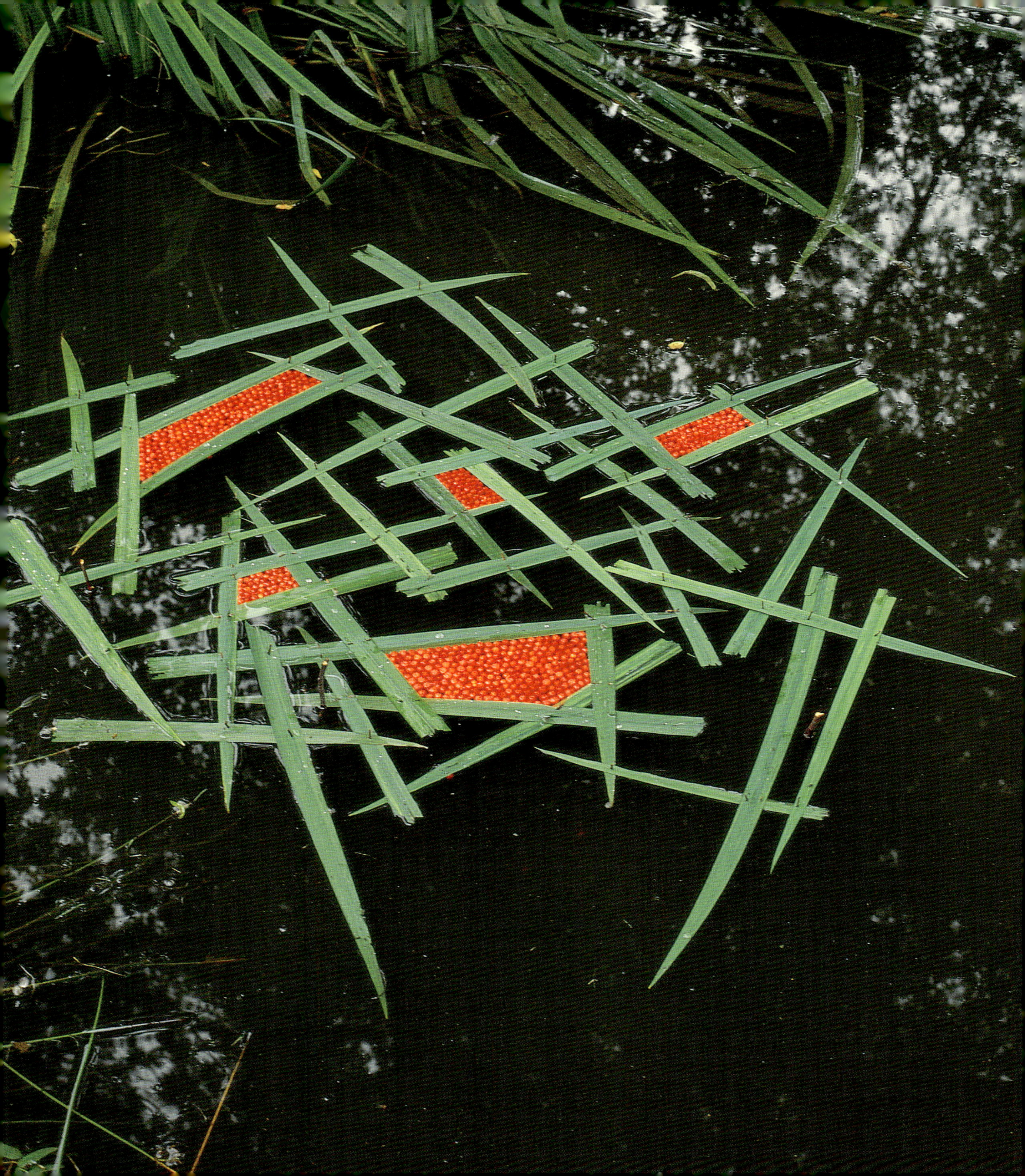

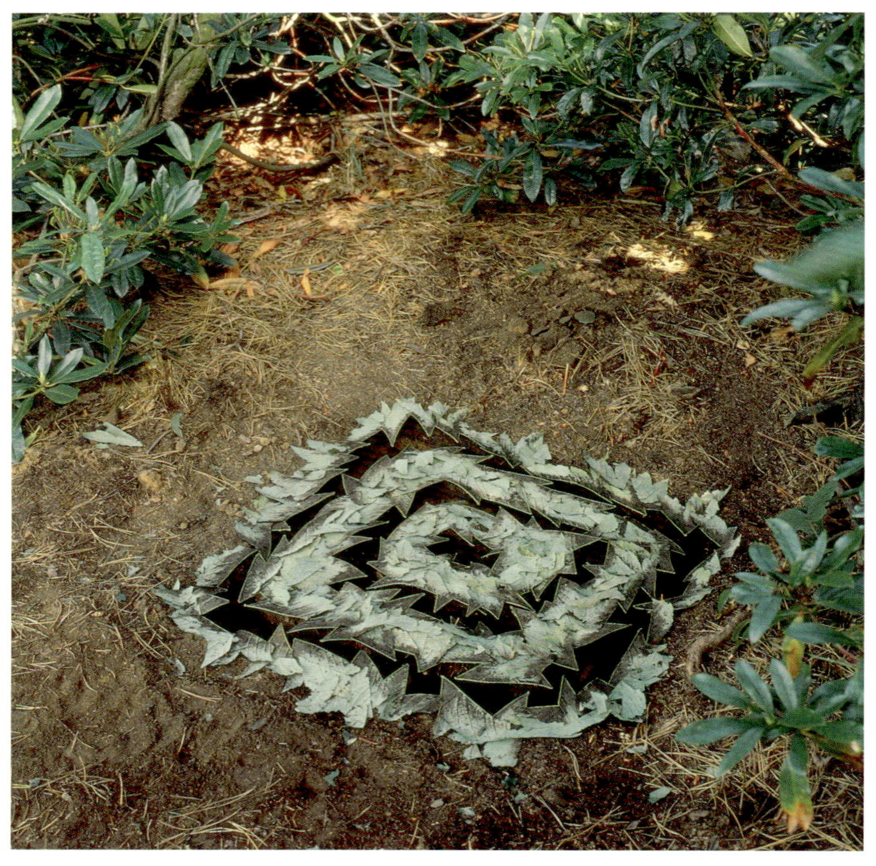

Sycamore leaf sections
torn along the veins
smeared with mud
laid alongside channels

31 AUGUST 1987

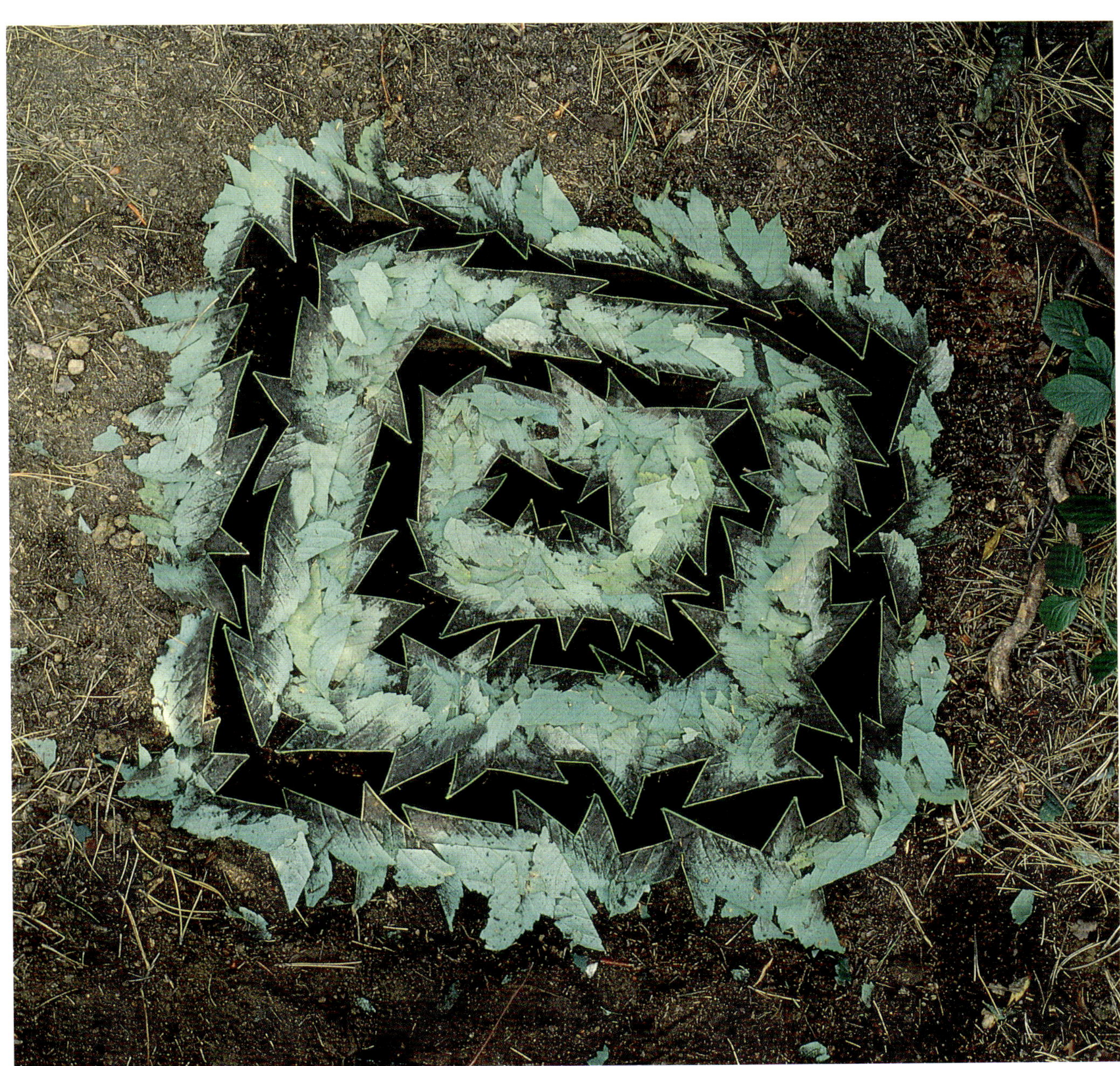

Sycamore leaf box
supported by its own architecture
stitched with thorns
moving with the breeze
for David Nash

4 SEPTEMBER 1987

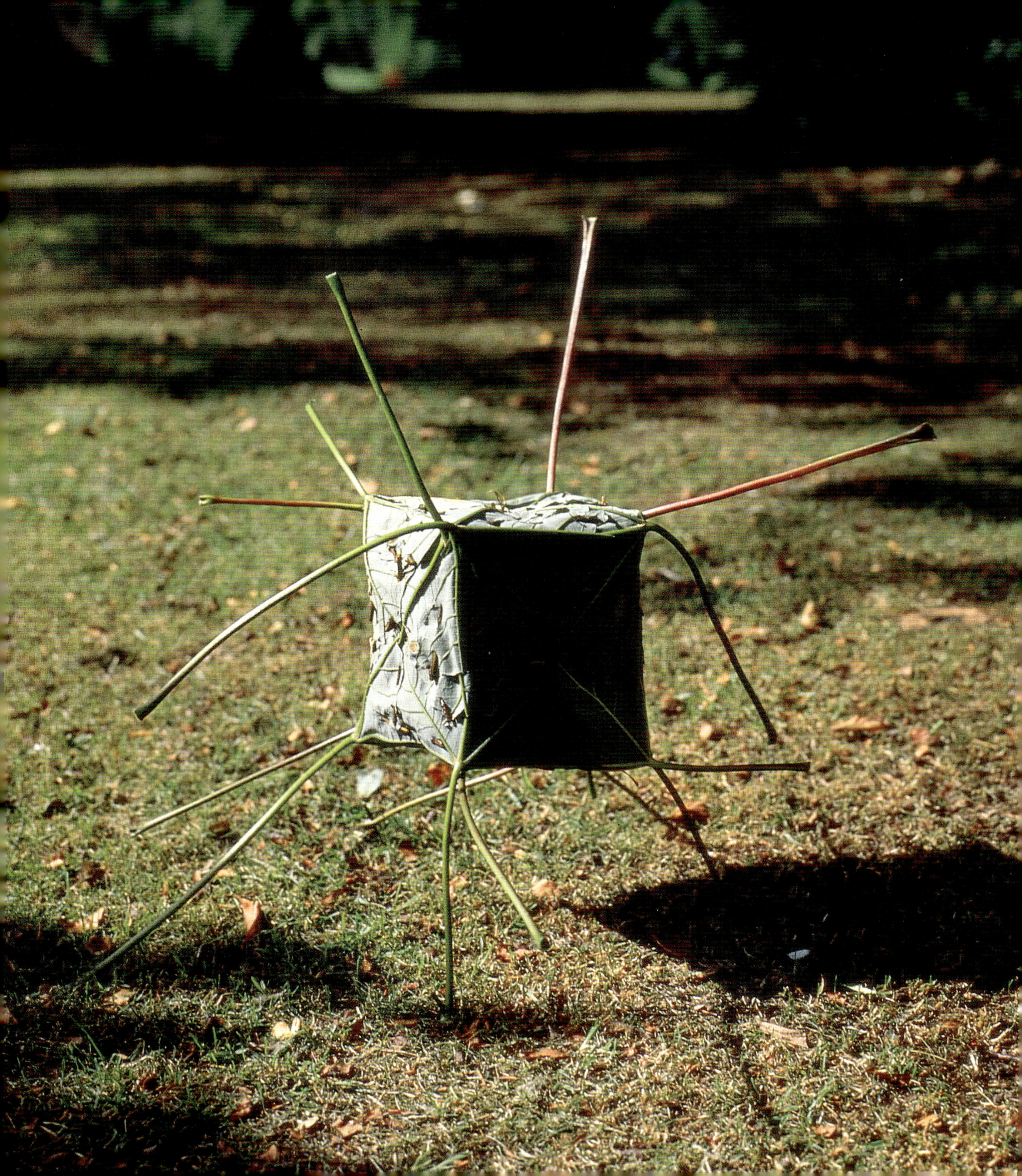

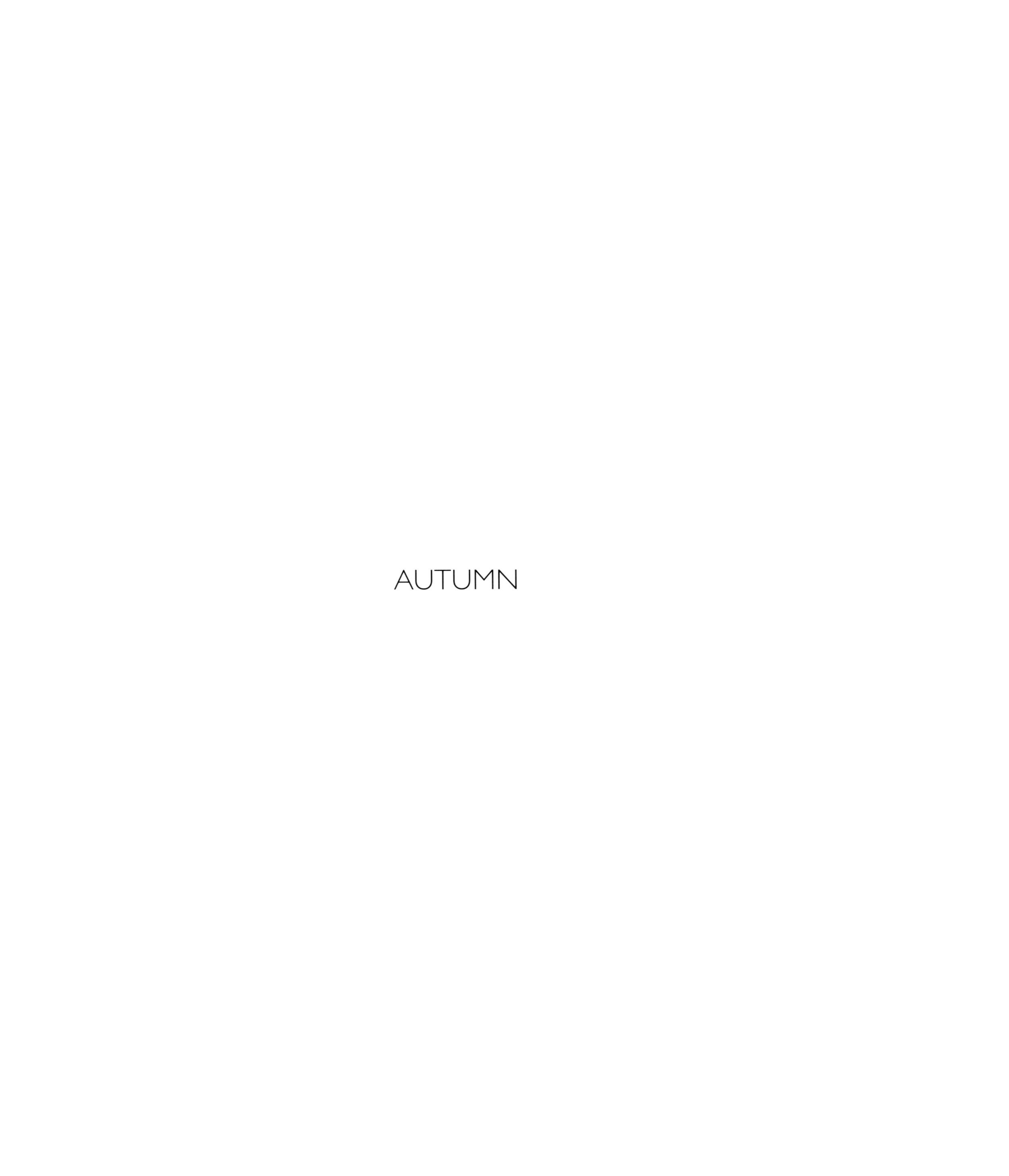

AUTUMN

Leaves on leaves
pressed flat with spit
windy
held to ground with stalks and thorns
streaks/lines to explore colour in horse chestnut

21, 22, 23 OCTOBER 1987

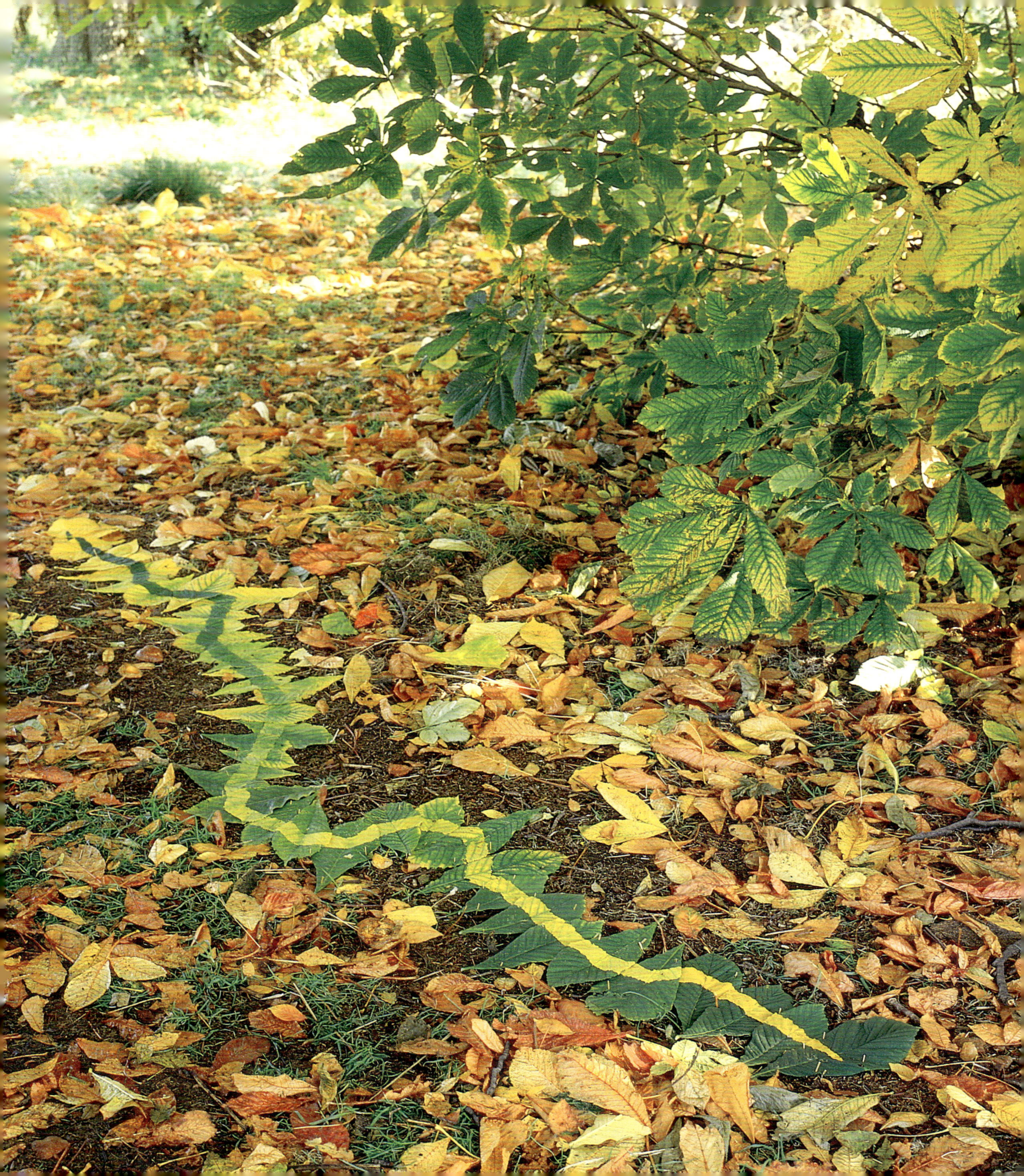

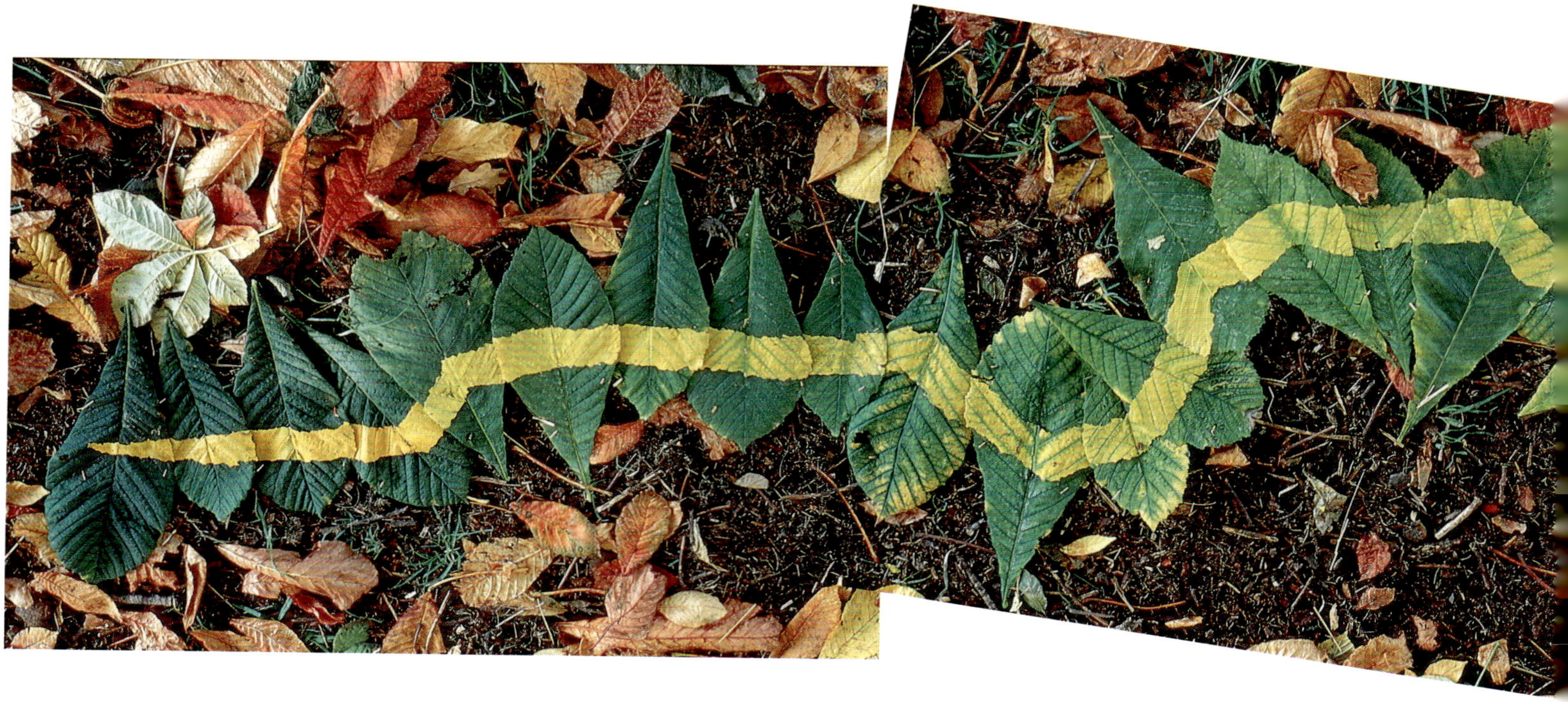

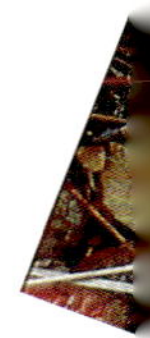

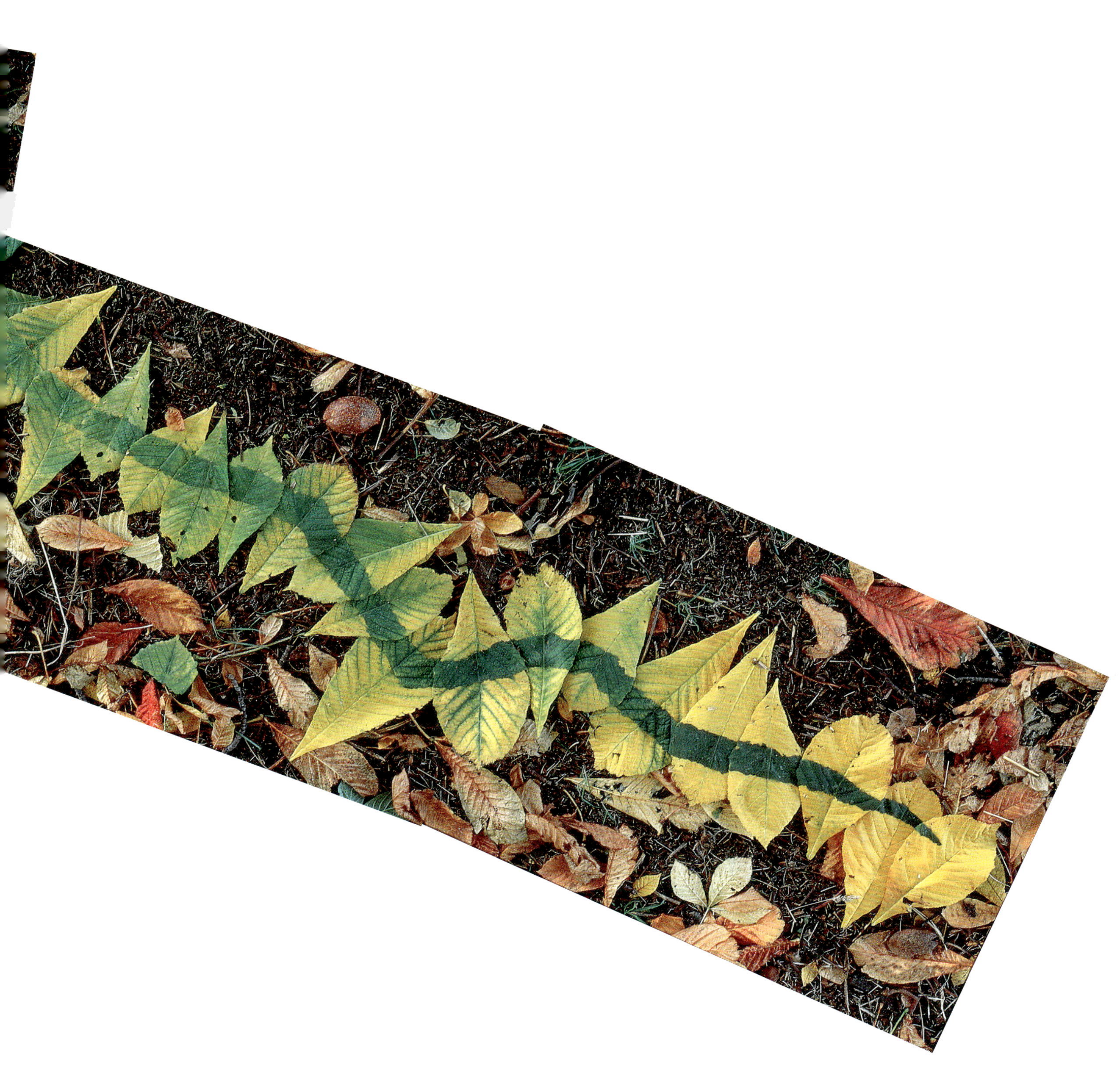

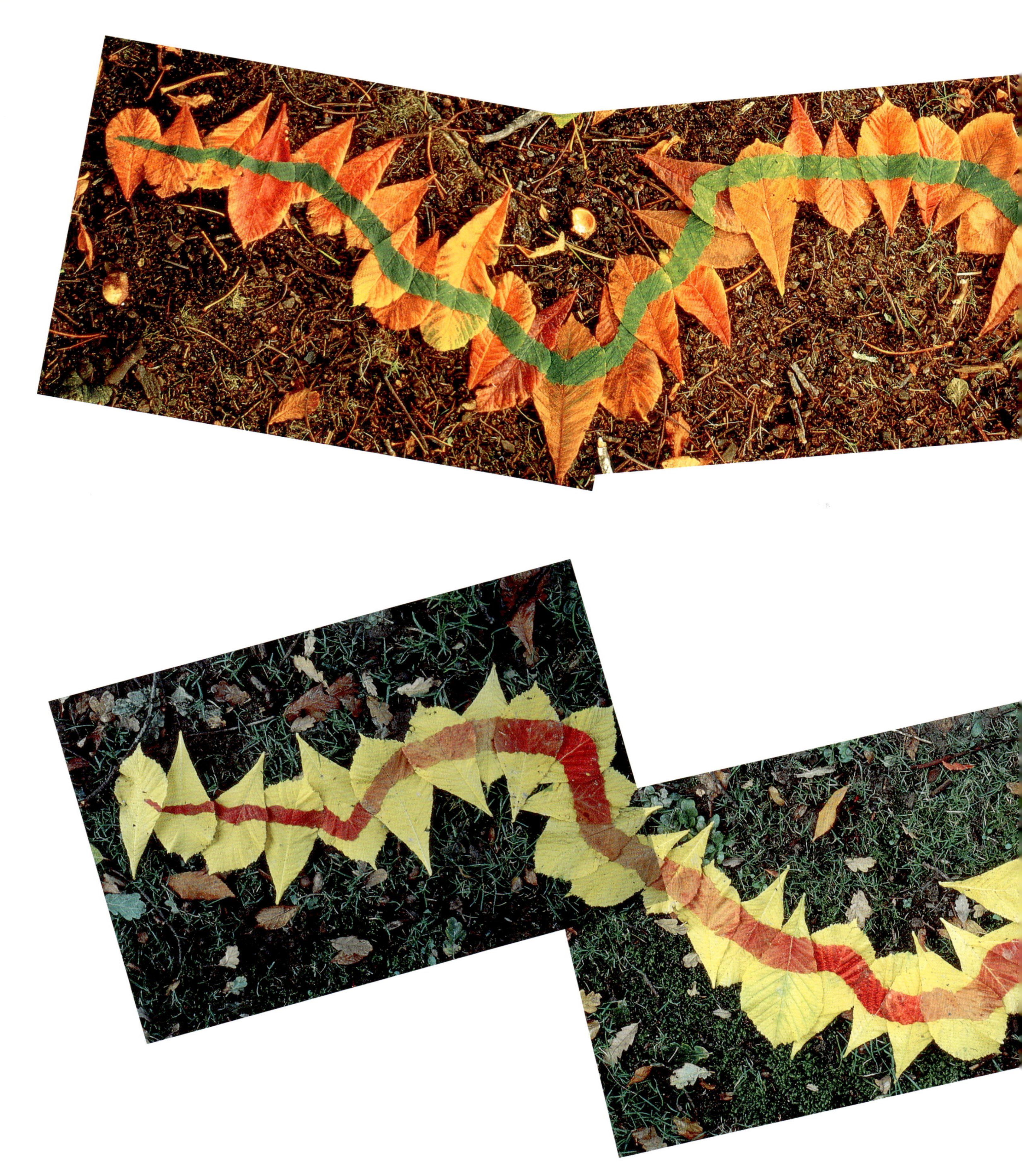

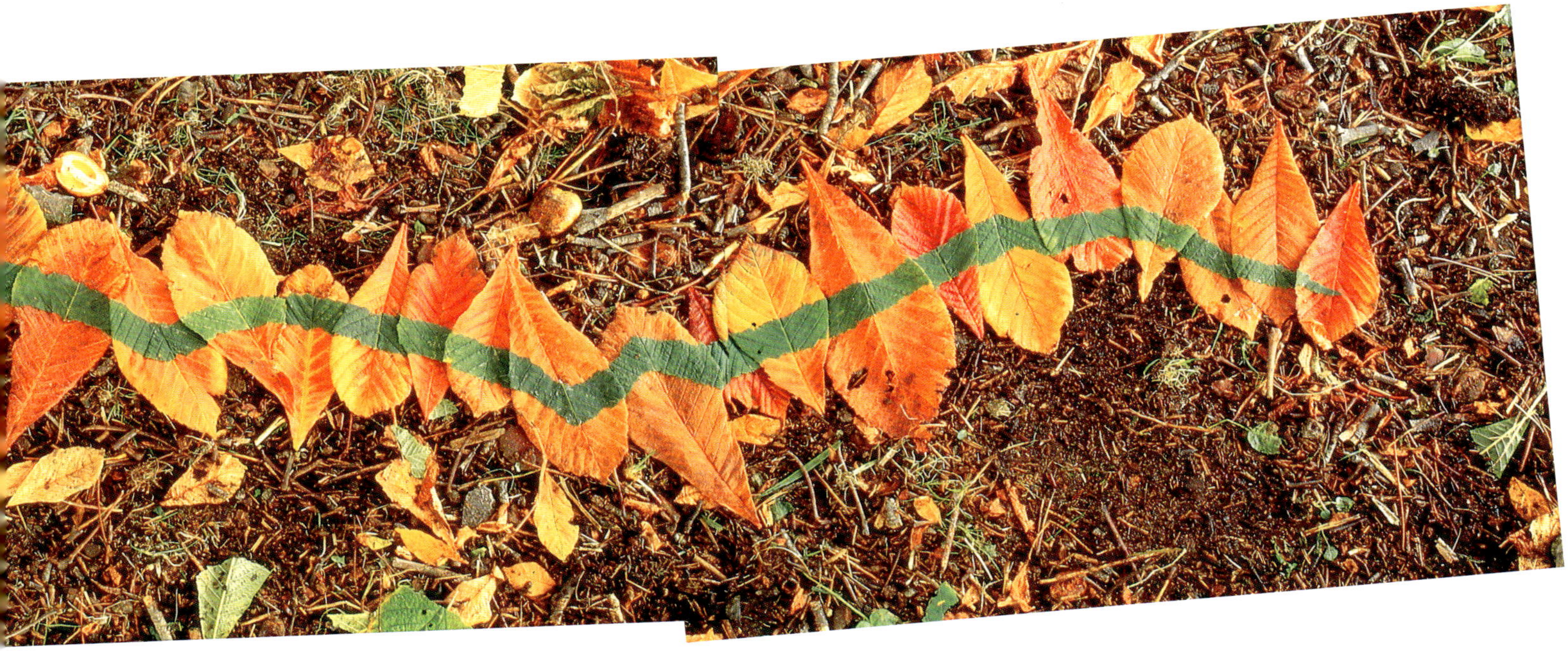

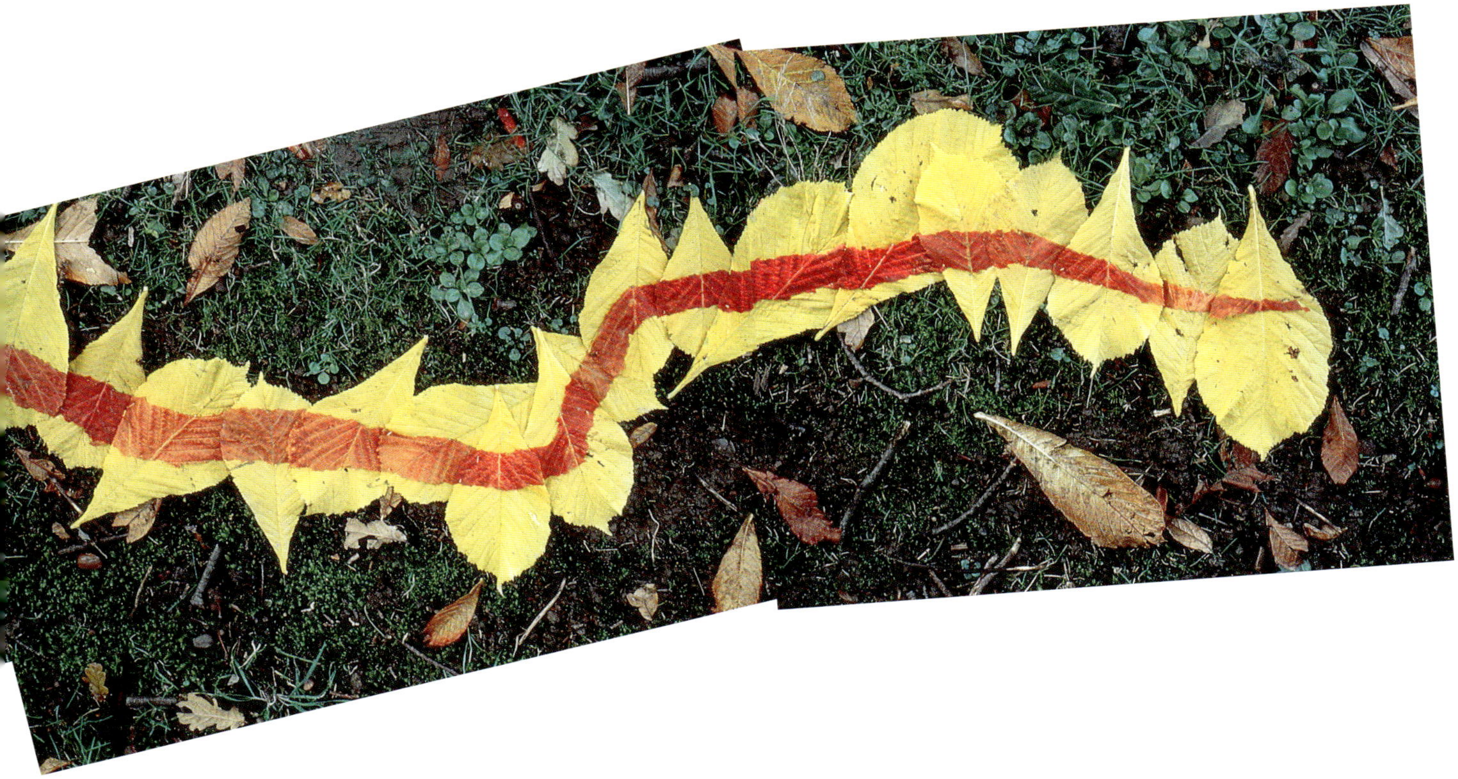

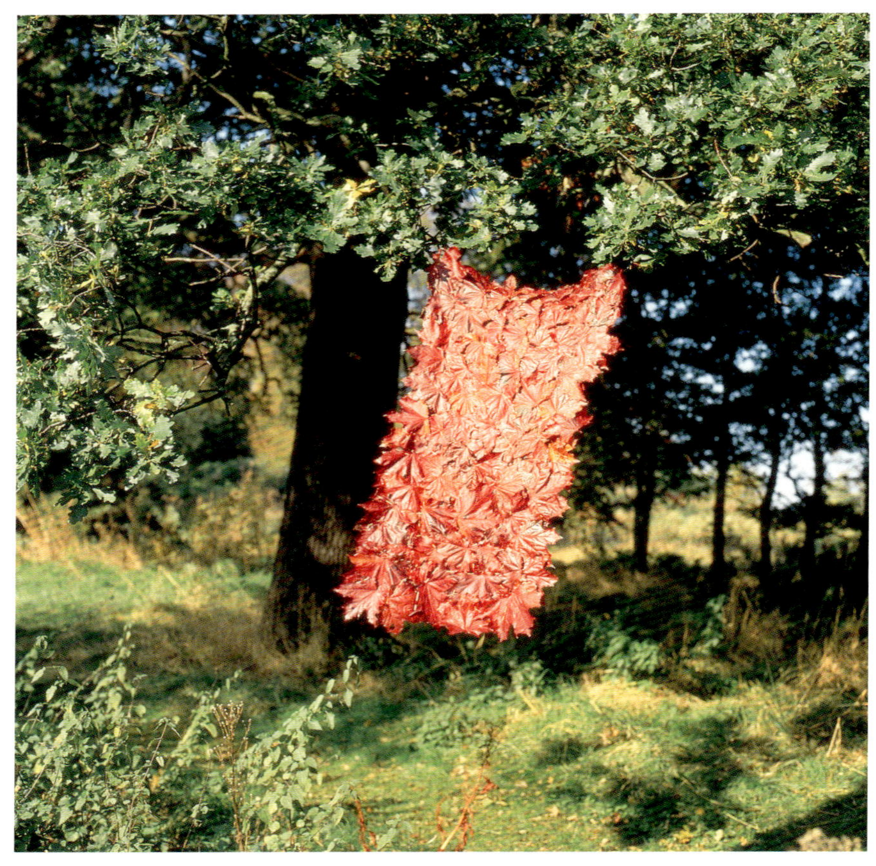

Sycamore leaves
stitched together with stalks
hung from a still green oak

23 OCTOBER 1987

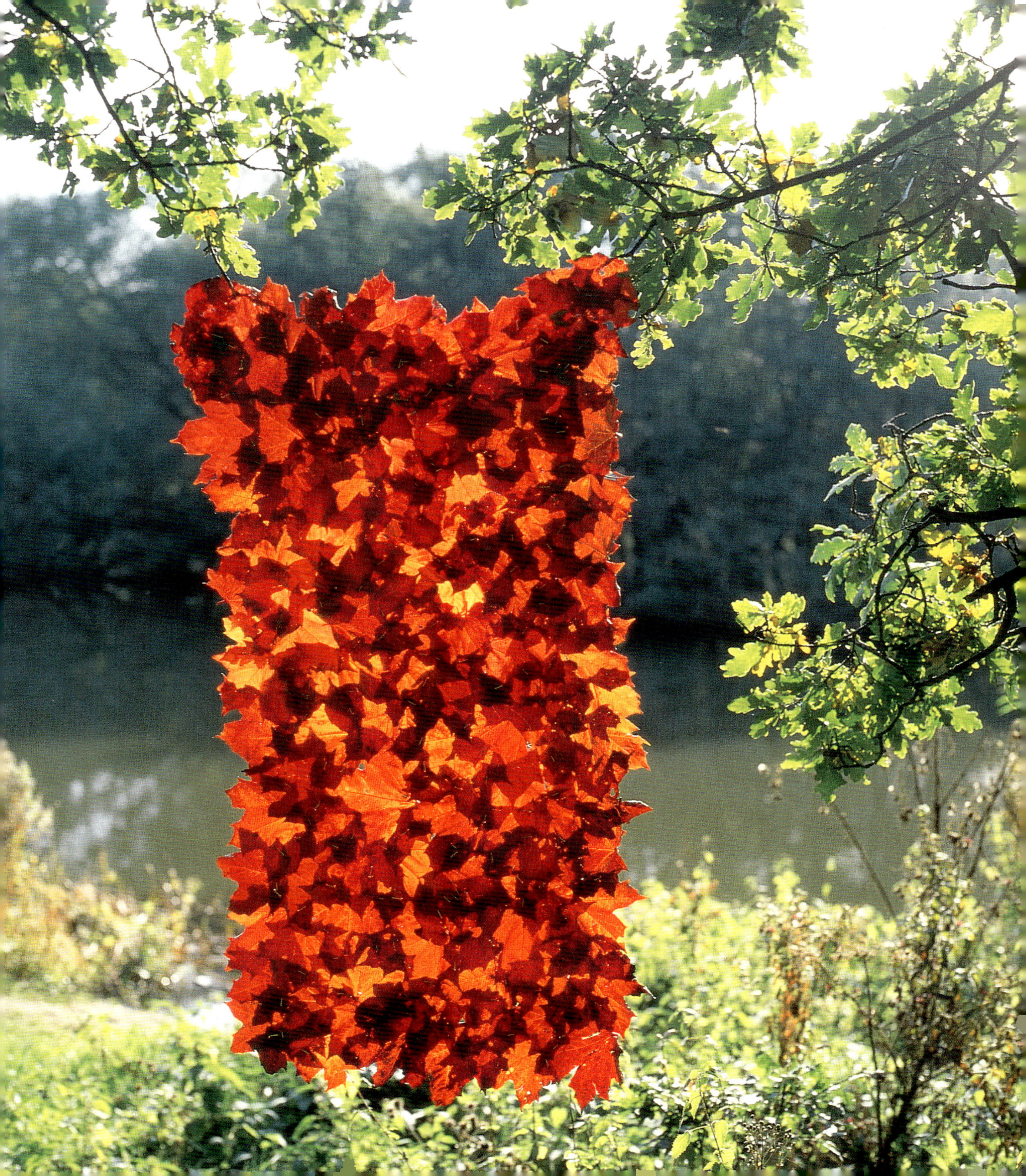

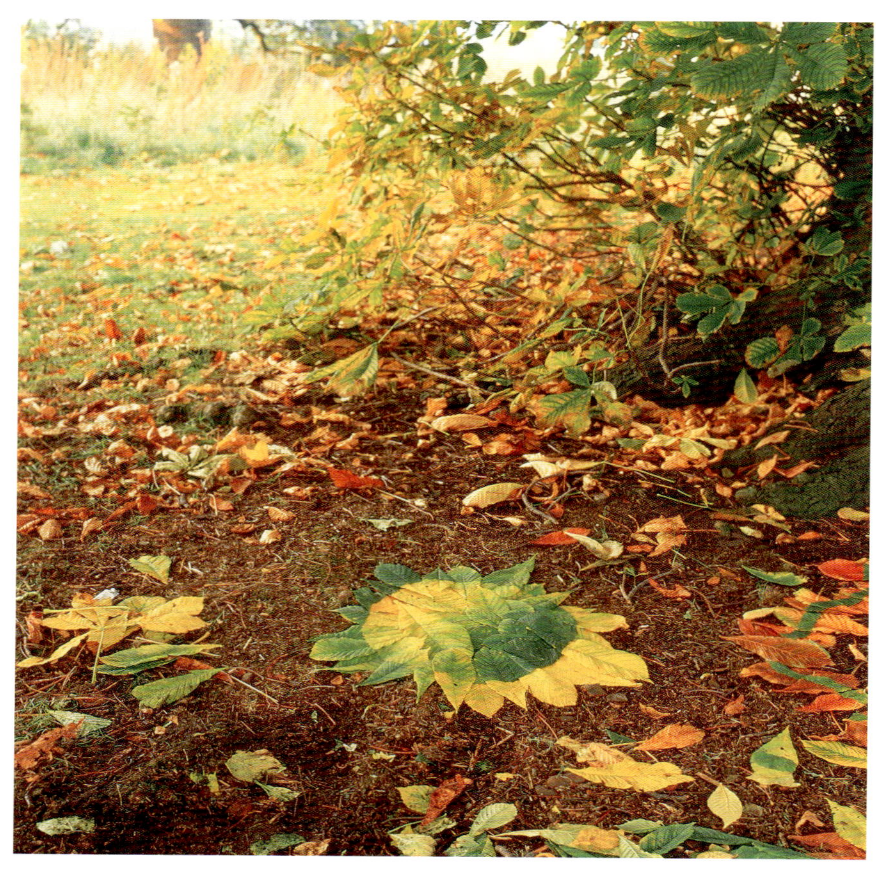

Horse chestnut patch
green to yellow
torn leaves
with spit

24 OCTOBER 1987

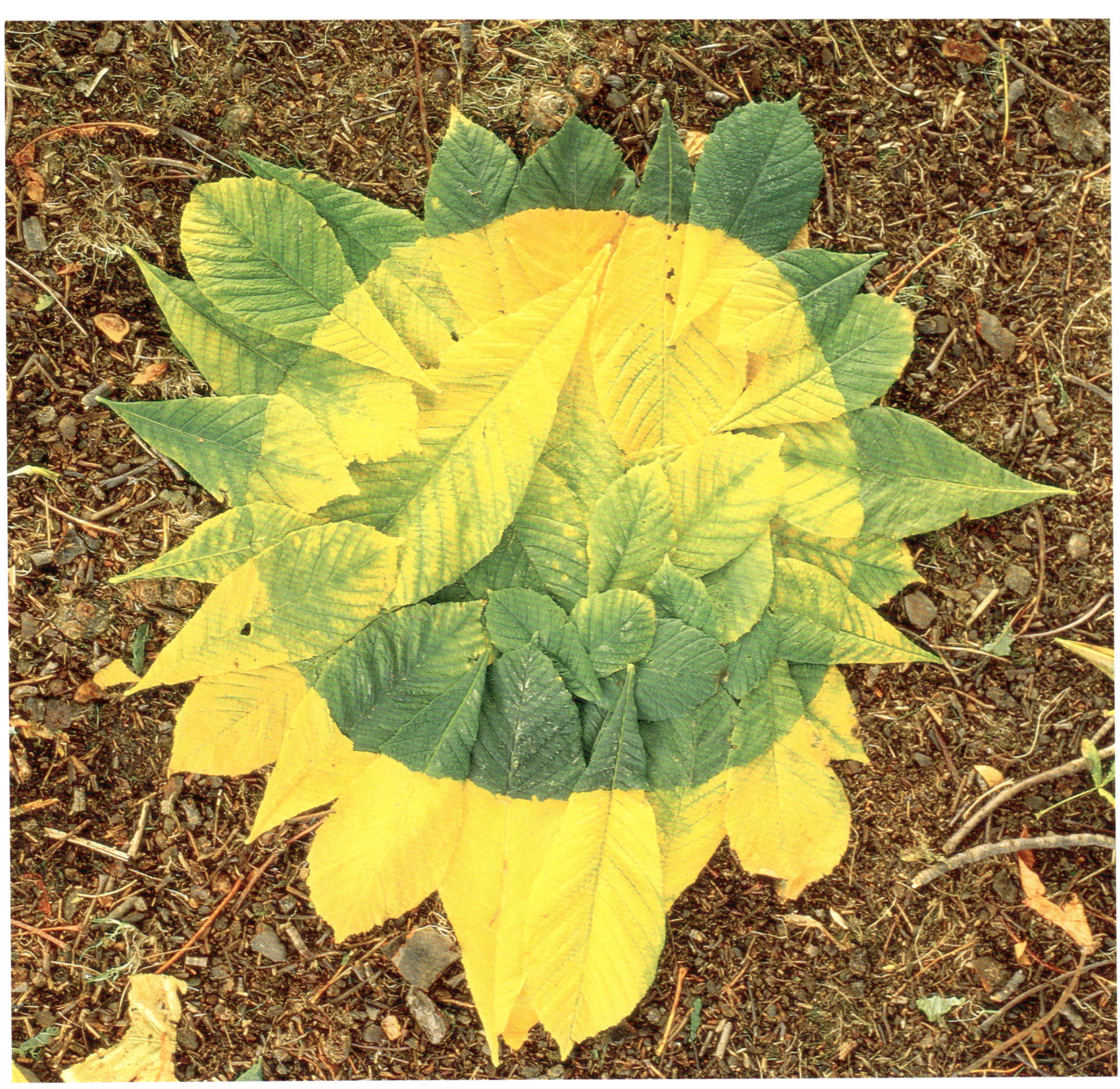

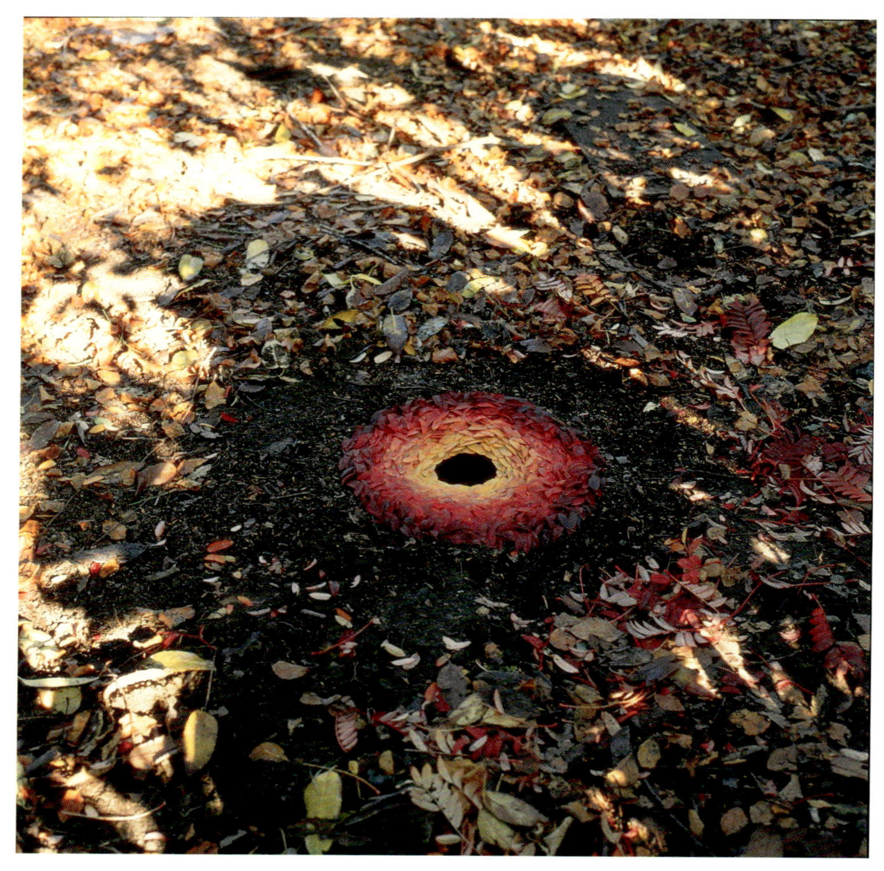

Rowan leaves laid around a hole
collecting the last few leaves
nearly finished
dog ran into hole
started again
made in the shadow of a sunny day
windy
sheltered by rhododendron bush

25 OCTOBER 1987

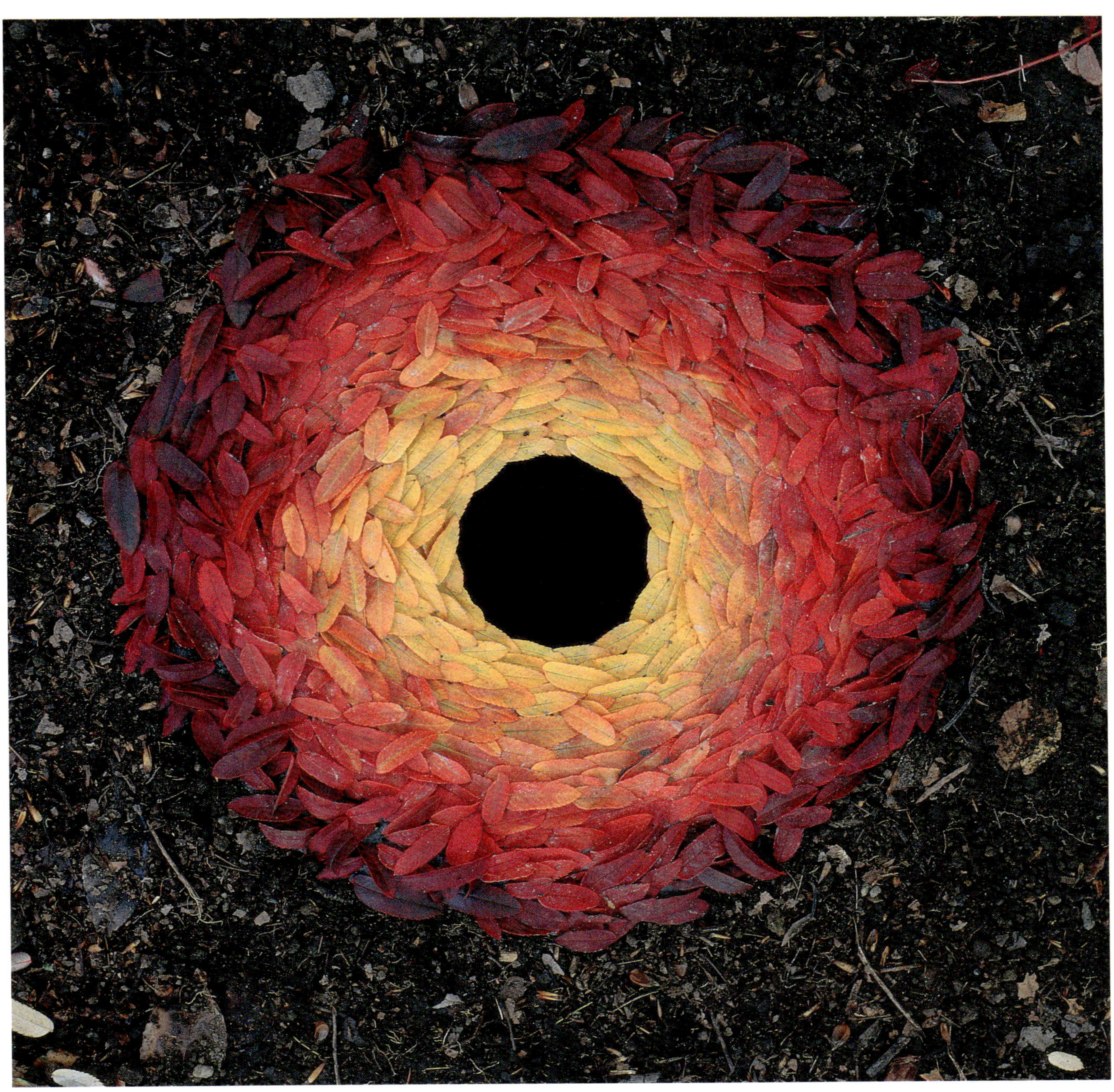

Sweet chestnut
autumn horn

28 OCTOBER 1987

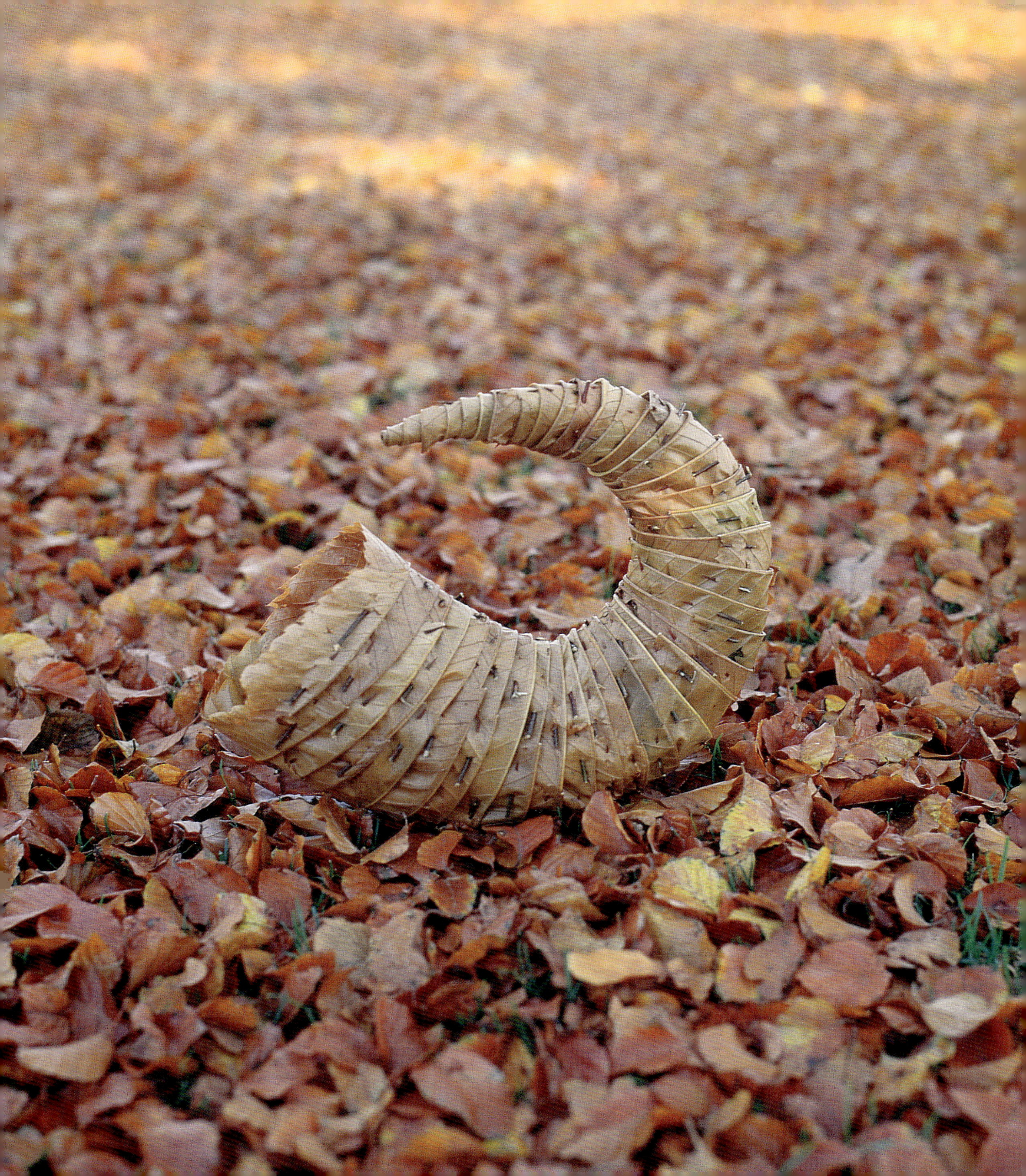

Trench
dug over two days
earth brought to an edge
clay supported with sticks
cold, darkly overcast but no rain
a hot day would have caused the clay to dry out
a wet day would have washed the earth away

6 AND 7 AUGUST 1987

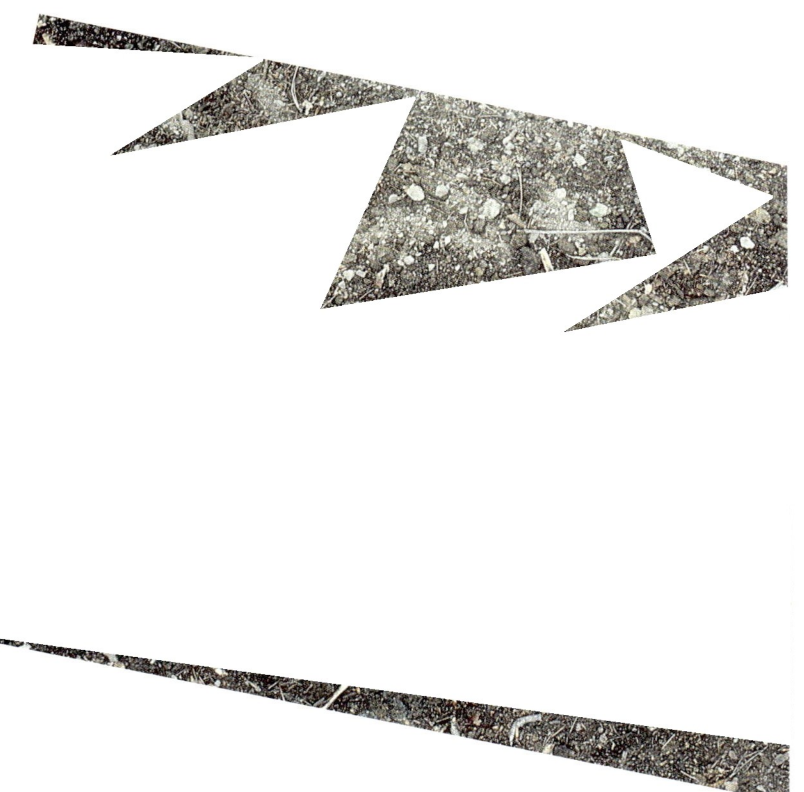

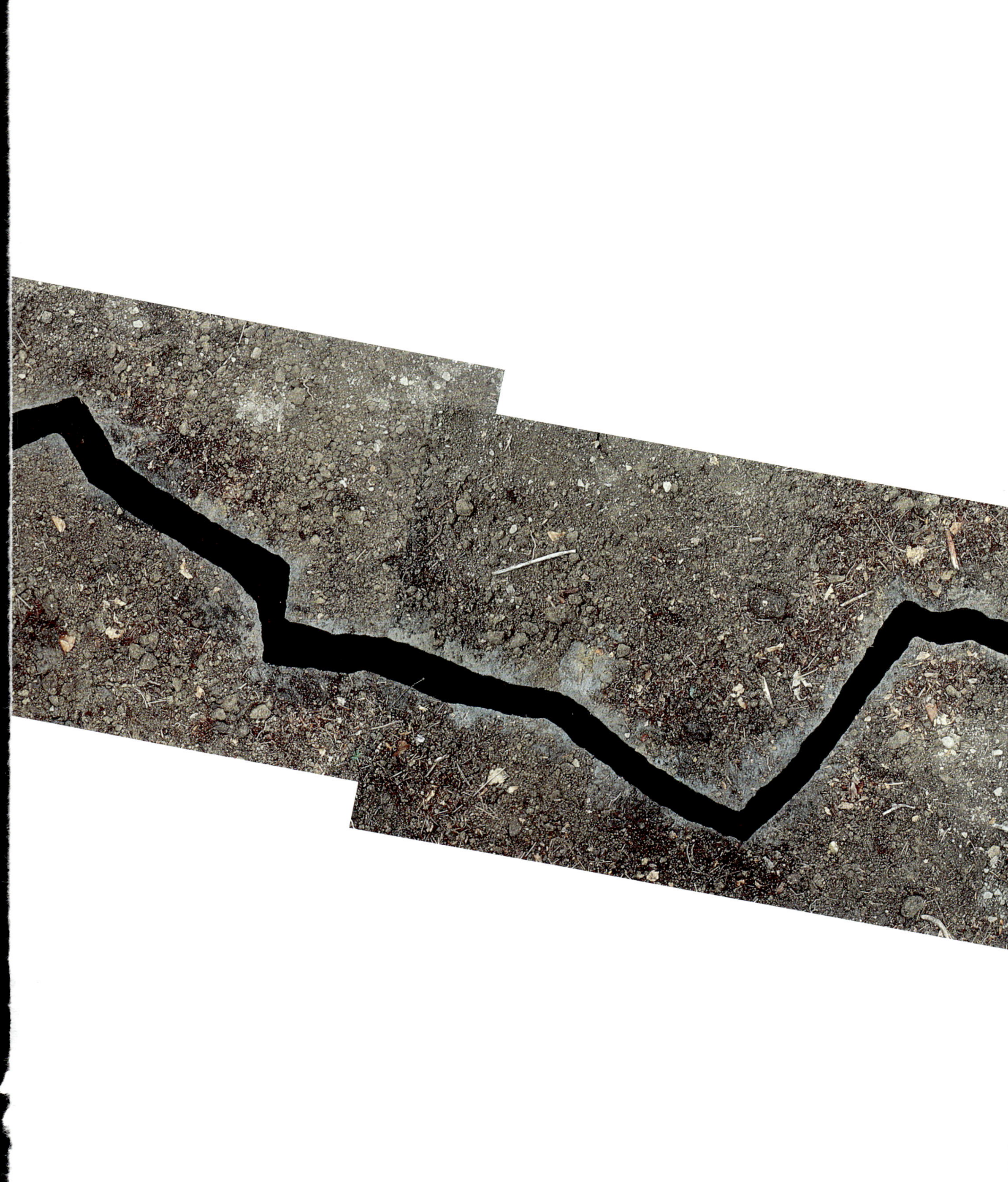

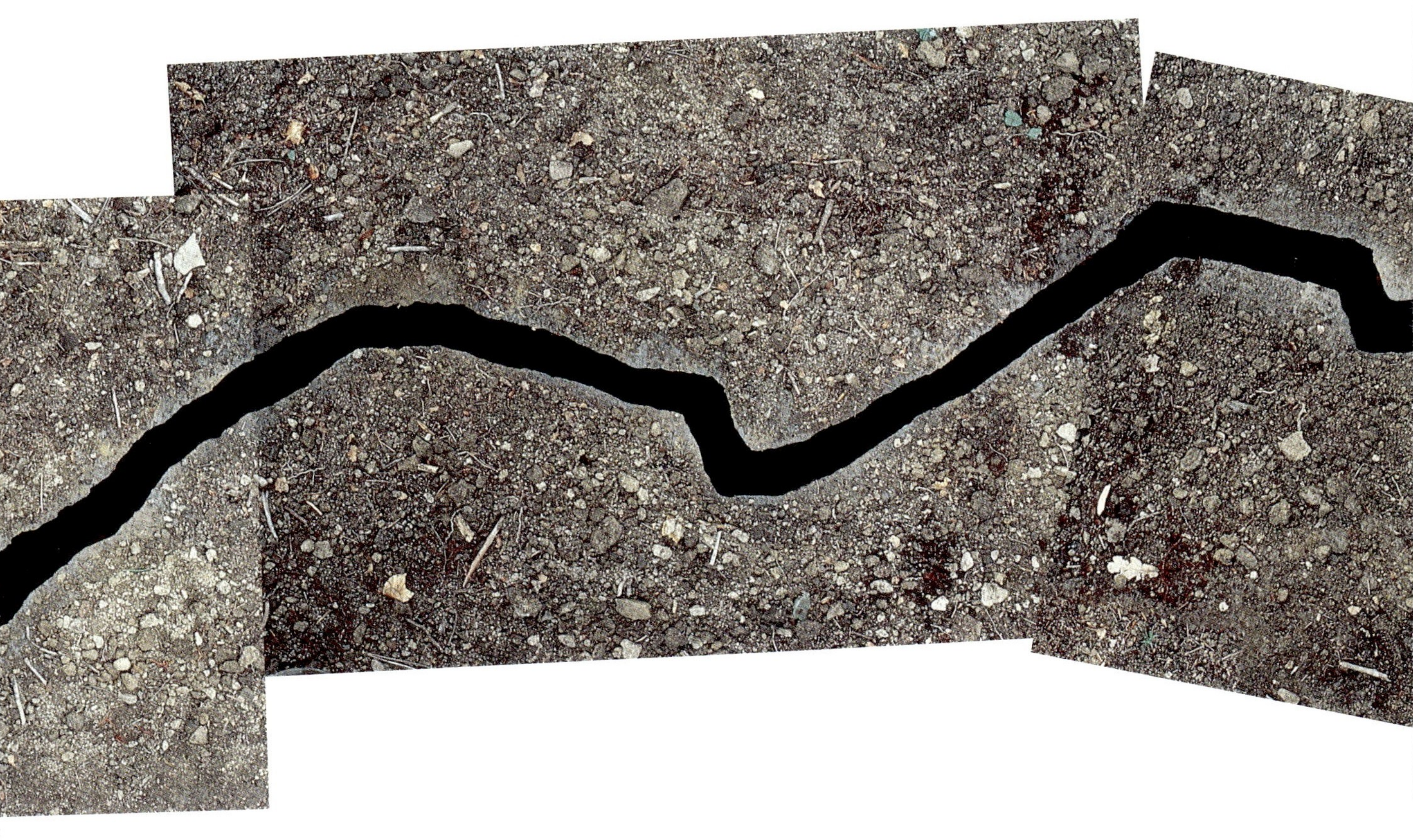

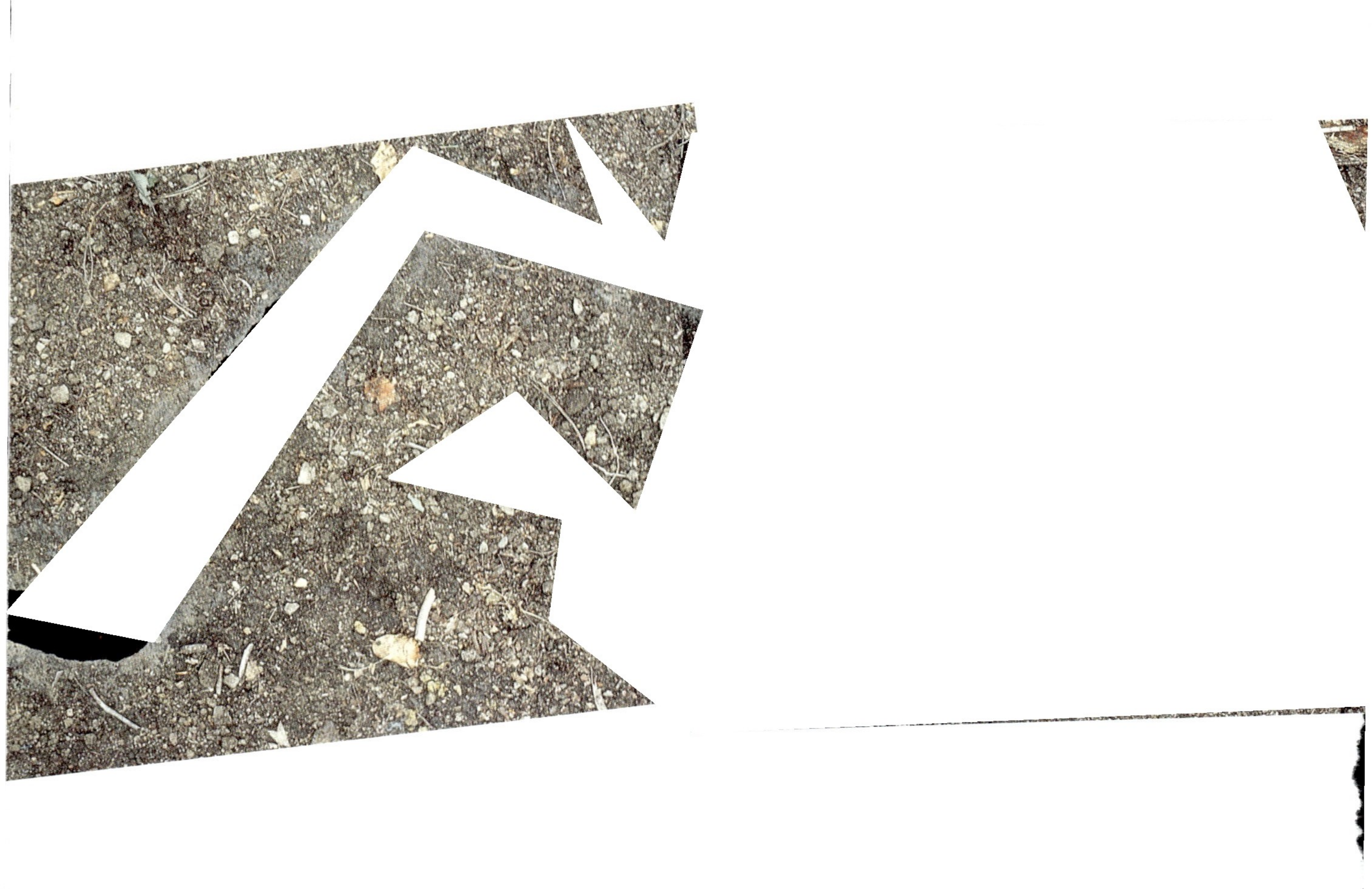

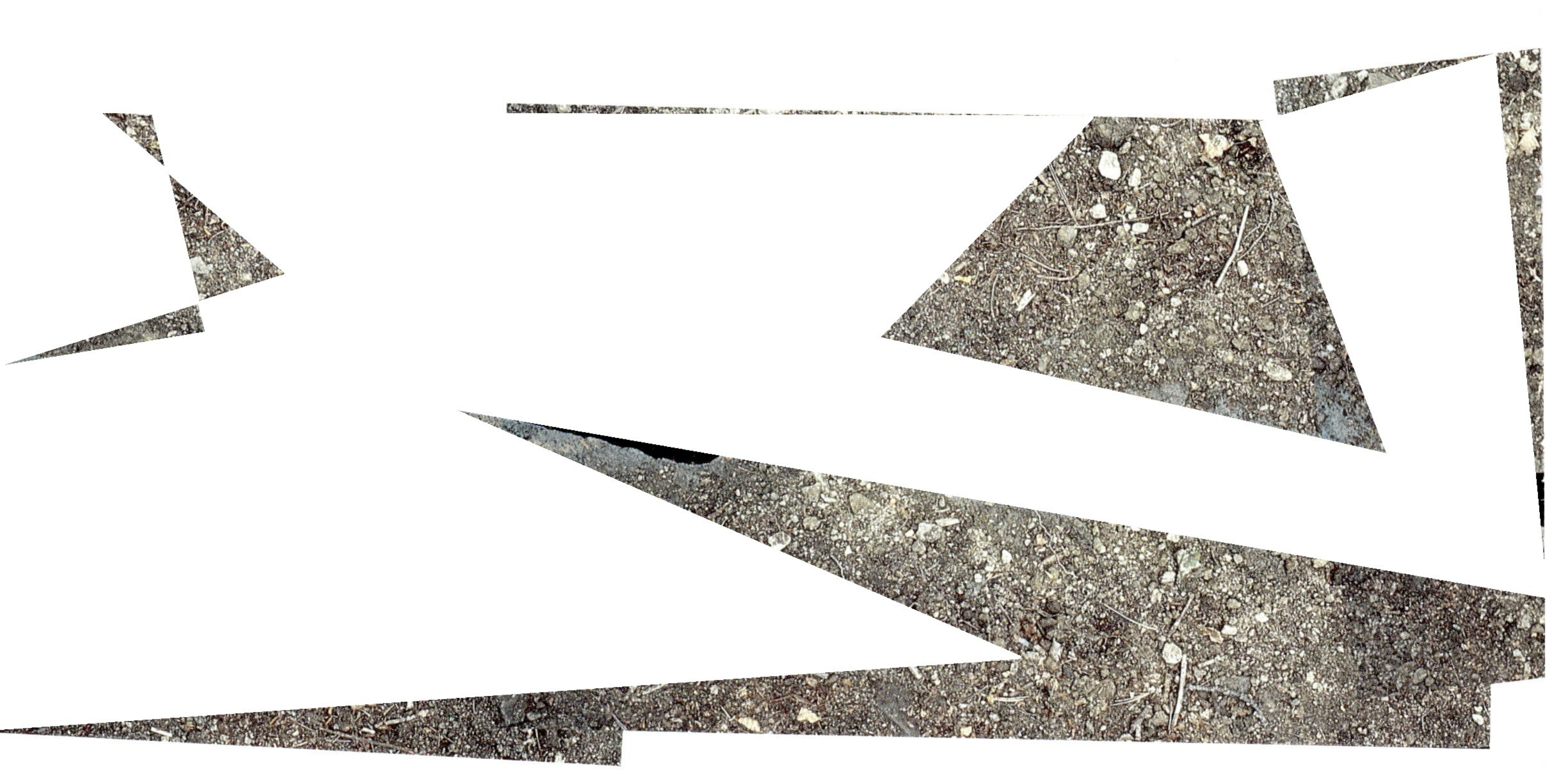